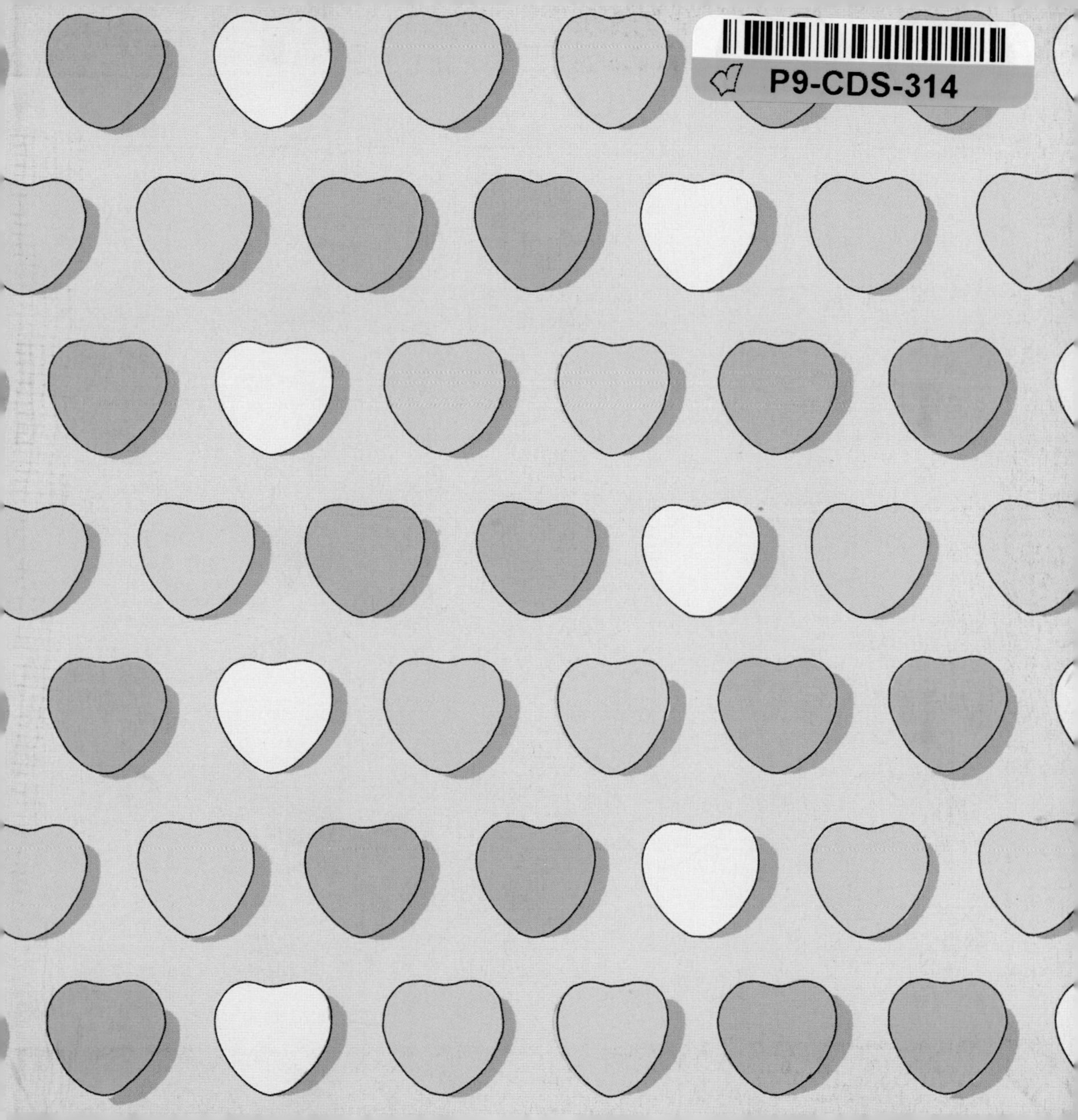

CANDY HEARTS

Andrews McMeel Publishing
a division of Andrews McMeel Universal
1130 Walnut Street, Kansas City, Missouri 64106

www.andrewsmcmeel.com

21 22 23 24 25 SDB 10 9 8 7 6 5 4 3 2 1

ISBN: 978-1-5248-6506-1

Library of Congress Control Number: 2020943987

Editor: Lucas Wetzel
Art Director: Diane Marsh
Production Editor: Amy Strassner
Production Manager: Tamara Haus

ATTENTION: SCHOOLS AND BUSINESSES
Andrews McMeel books are available at quantity discounts with
bulk purchase for educational, business, or sales promotional use.
For information, please e-mail the Andrews McMeel Publishing
Special Sales Department: specialsales@amuniversal.com.

CANDY HEARTS

TOMMY SIEGEL

Andrews McMeel
PUBLISHING®

INTRODUCTION

On Valentine's Day, 2018, hundreds of days deep into a project in which I drew a comic every day for 500 days, I hastily whipped up a comic featuring conversation hearts on a date in a movie theater. A week later, another idea for a candy hearts comic came to mind. And then another. I started to realize that candy hearts made for a pretty convenient setup to illustrate inner monologues . . . on the outside. A way to cut to the truth and bluntly show what people are feeling but not expressing to their loved ones. At this point, I should clarify: I am not a psychologist or a licensed therapist, just a guy who draws candy hearts and dinosaurs with big butts on the internet. So try not to take these comics too seriously. I have a lot more I could say about what I've personally learned from thinking about the hidden inner lives of relationships, but I think I'll let the hearts speak for themselves — and continue telling the rest to my therapist. I hope you enjoy this collection of expressionless, walking hearts as much as I've enjoyed drawing them.

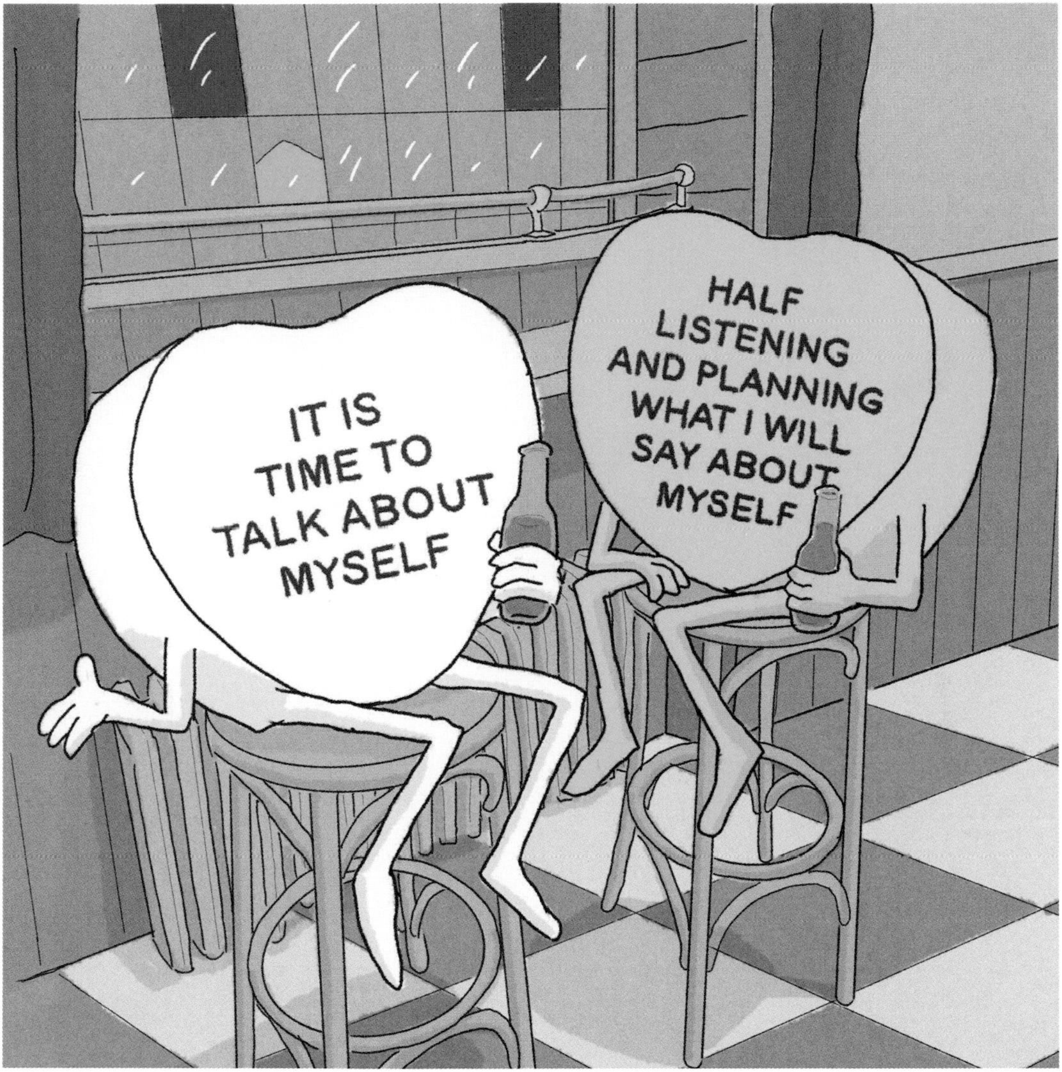
IT IS TIME TO TALK ABOUT MYSELF
HALF LISTENING AND PLANNING WHAT I WILL SAY ABOUT MYSELF

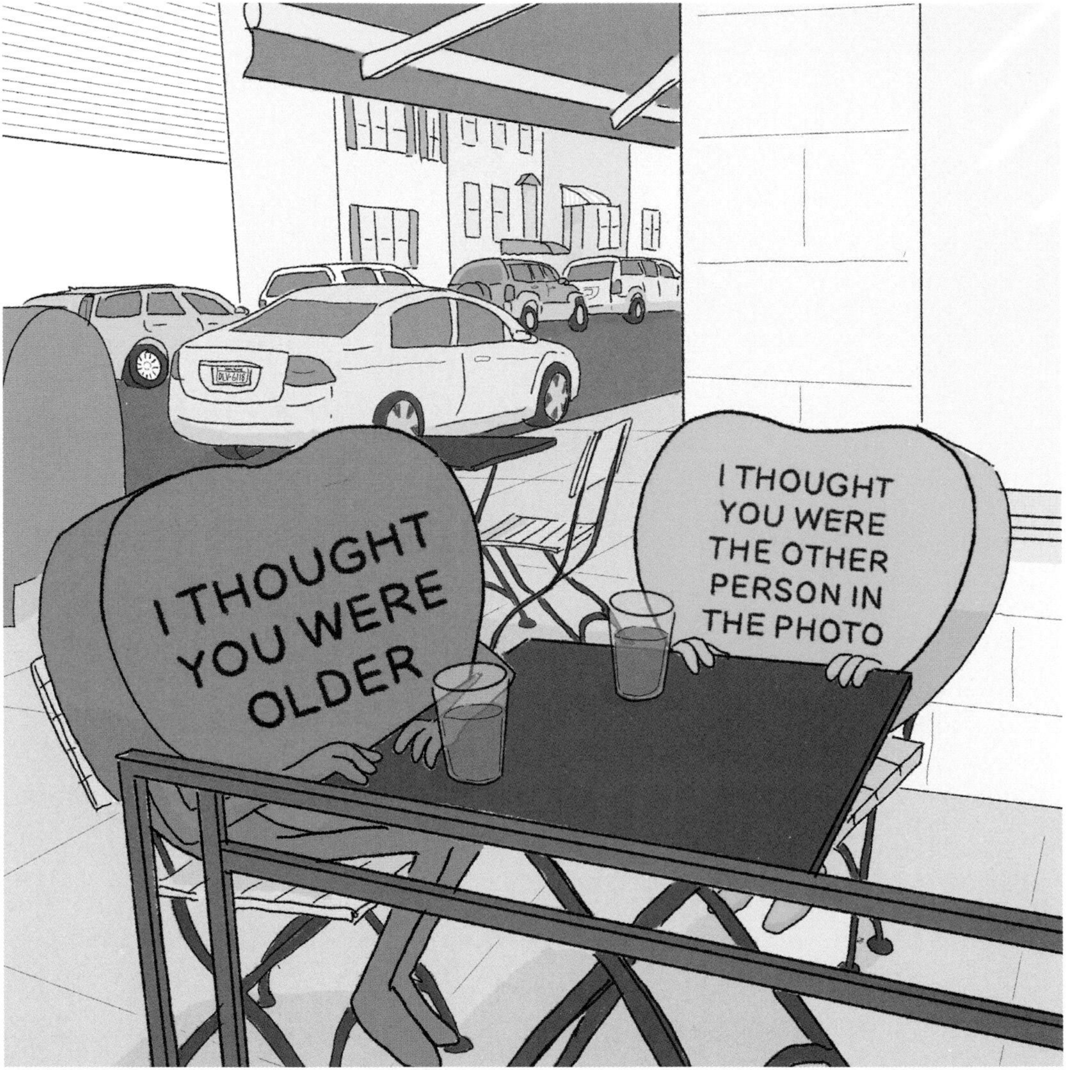
I THOUGHT YOU WERE OLDER
I THOUGHT YOU WERE THE OTHER PERSON IN THE PHOTO

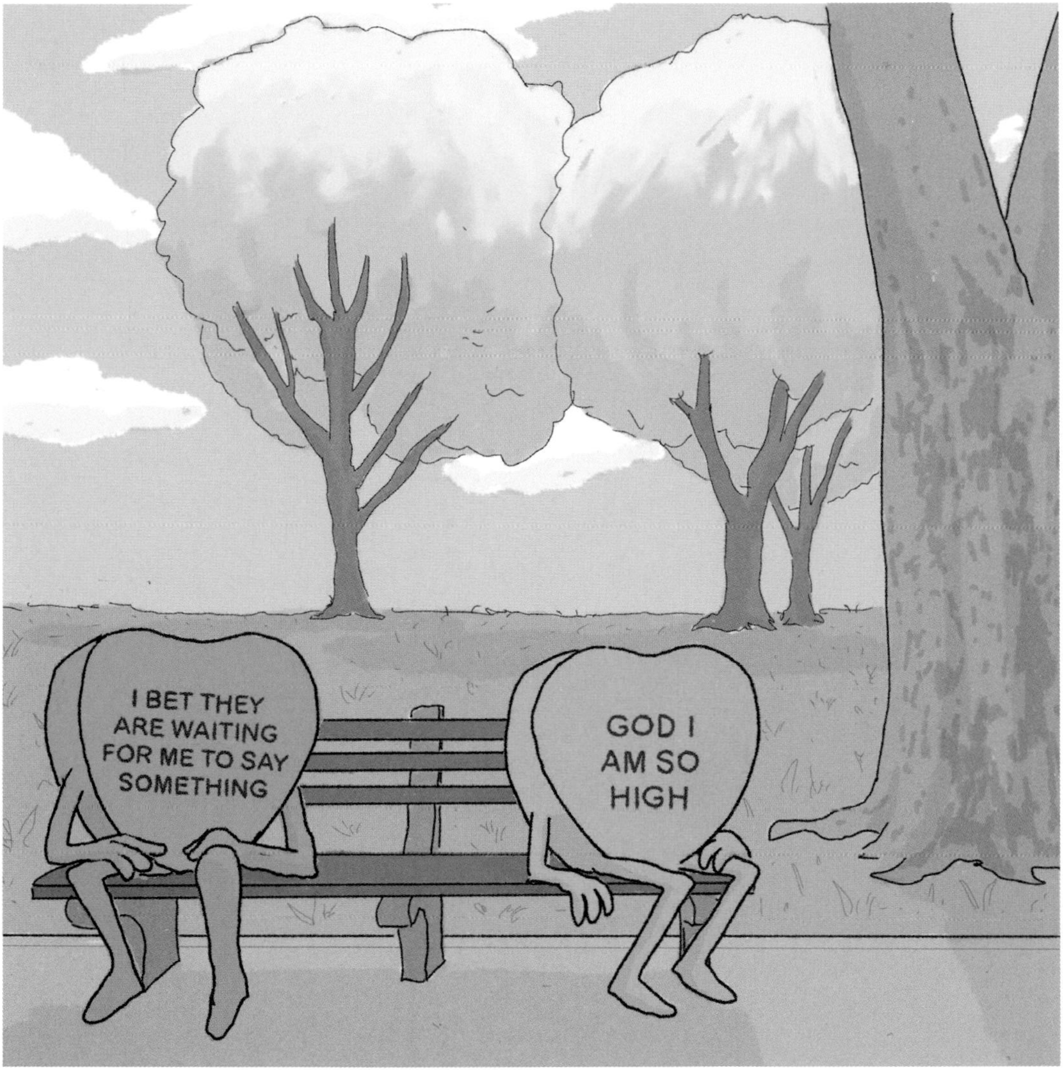
I BET THEY ARE WAITING FOR ME TO SAY SOMETHING
GOD I AM SO HIGH

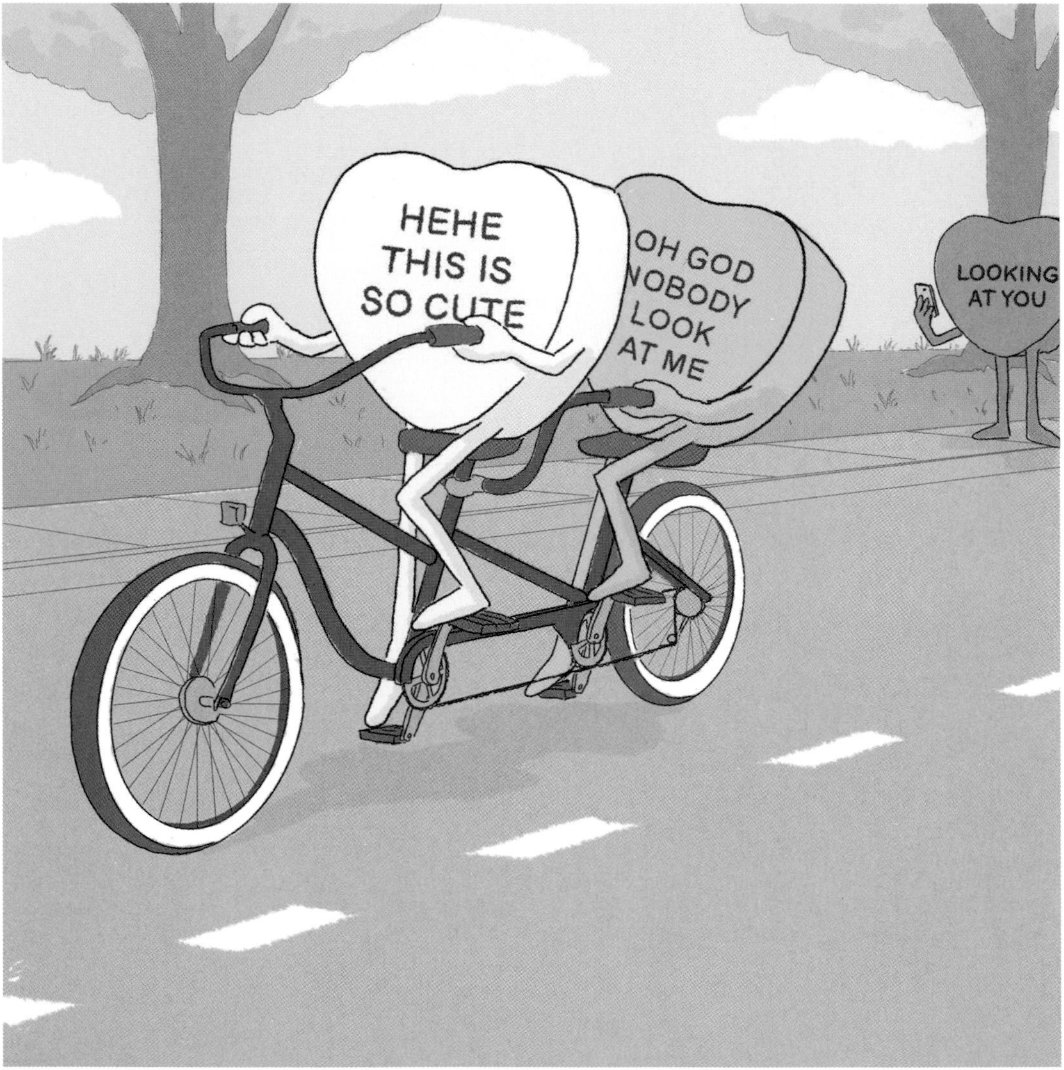
HEHE
THIS IS
SO CUTE
OH GOD
NOBODY
LOOK
AT ME
LOOKING
AT YOU

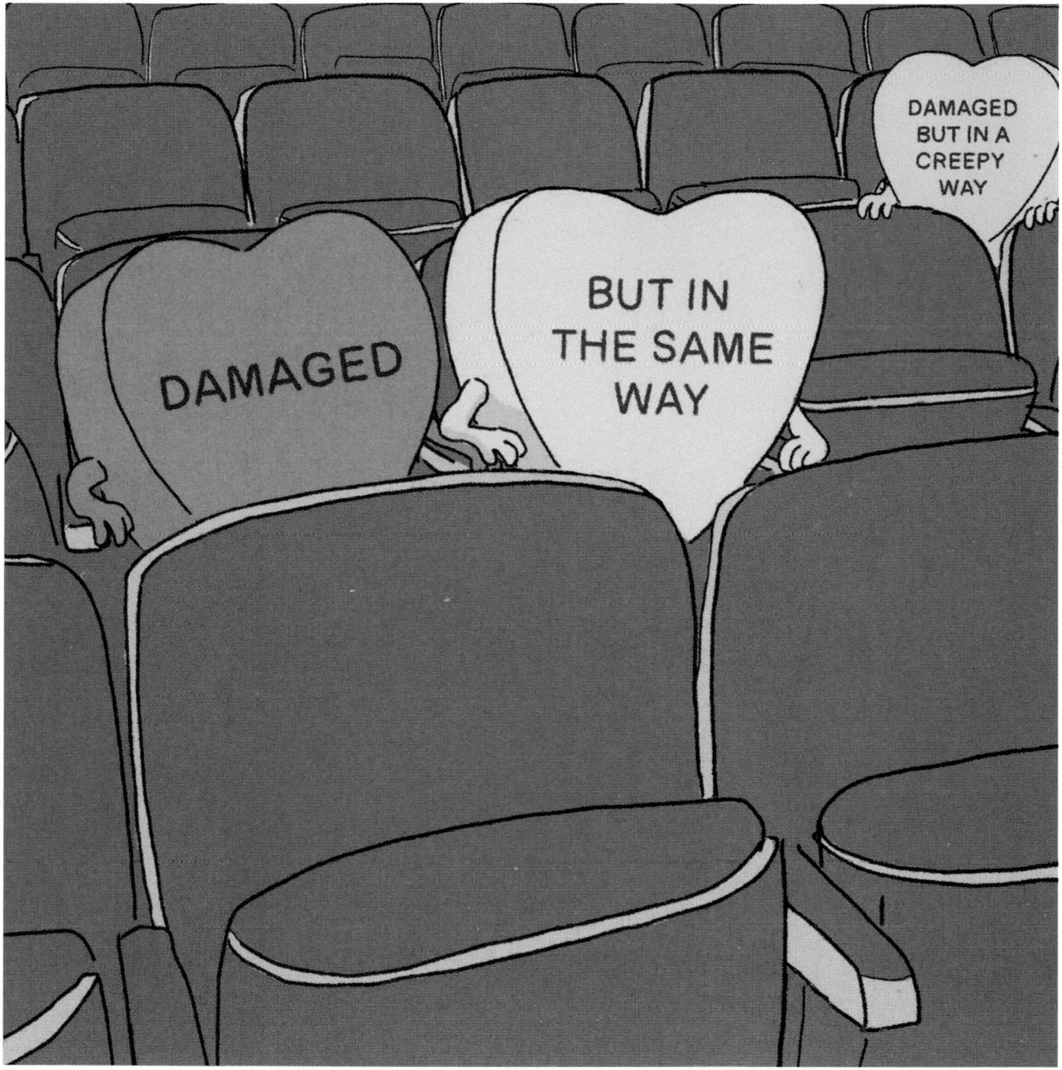
DAMAGED
BUT IN
THE SAME
WAY
DAMAGED
BUT IN A
CREEPY
WAY

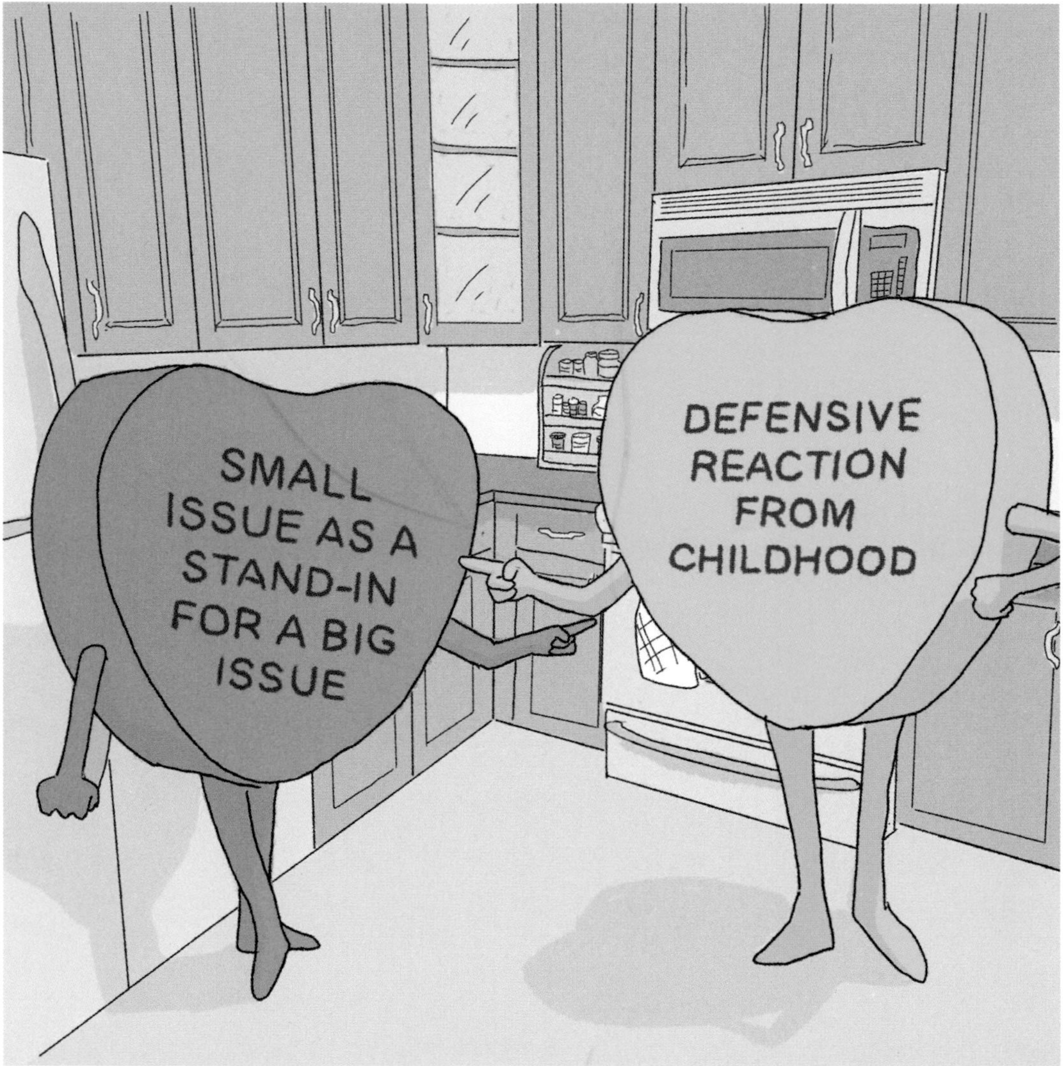
SMALL
ISSUE AS A
STAND-IN
FOR A BIG
ISSUE
DEFENSIVE
REACTION
FROM
CHILDHOOD

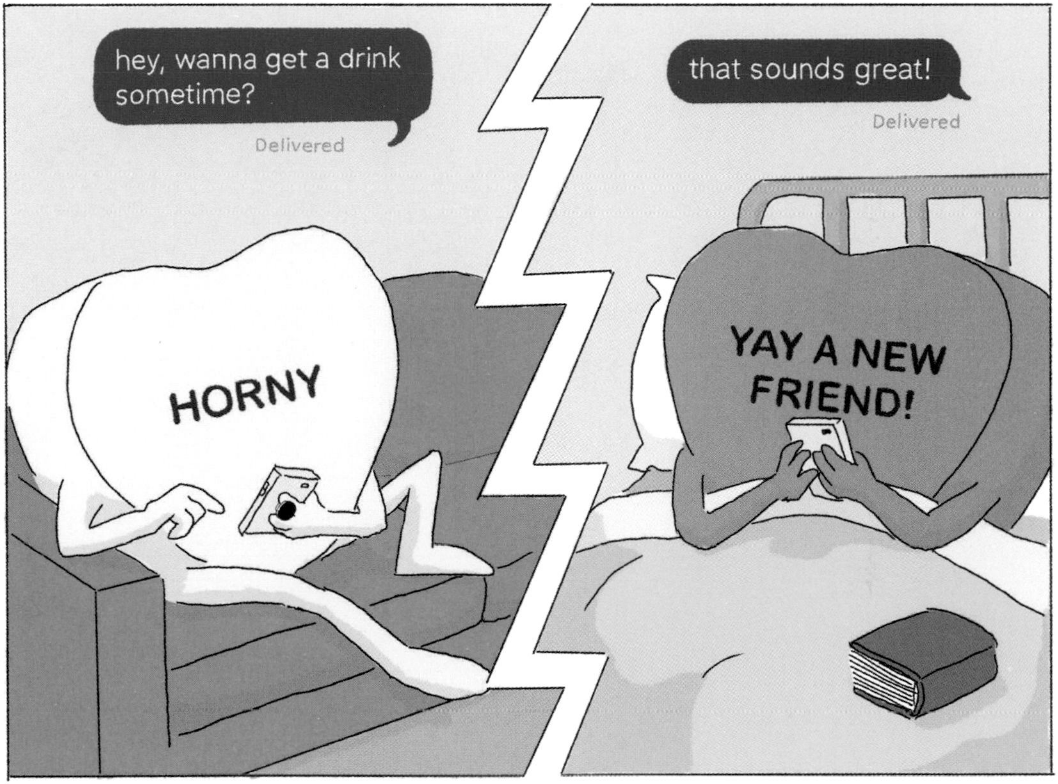
hey, wanna get a drink sometime?
Delivered
HORNY
that sounds great!
Delivered
YAY A NEW FRIEND!

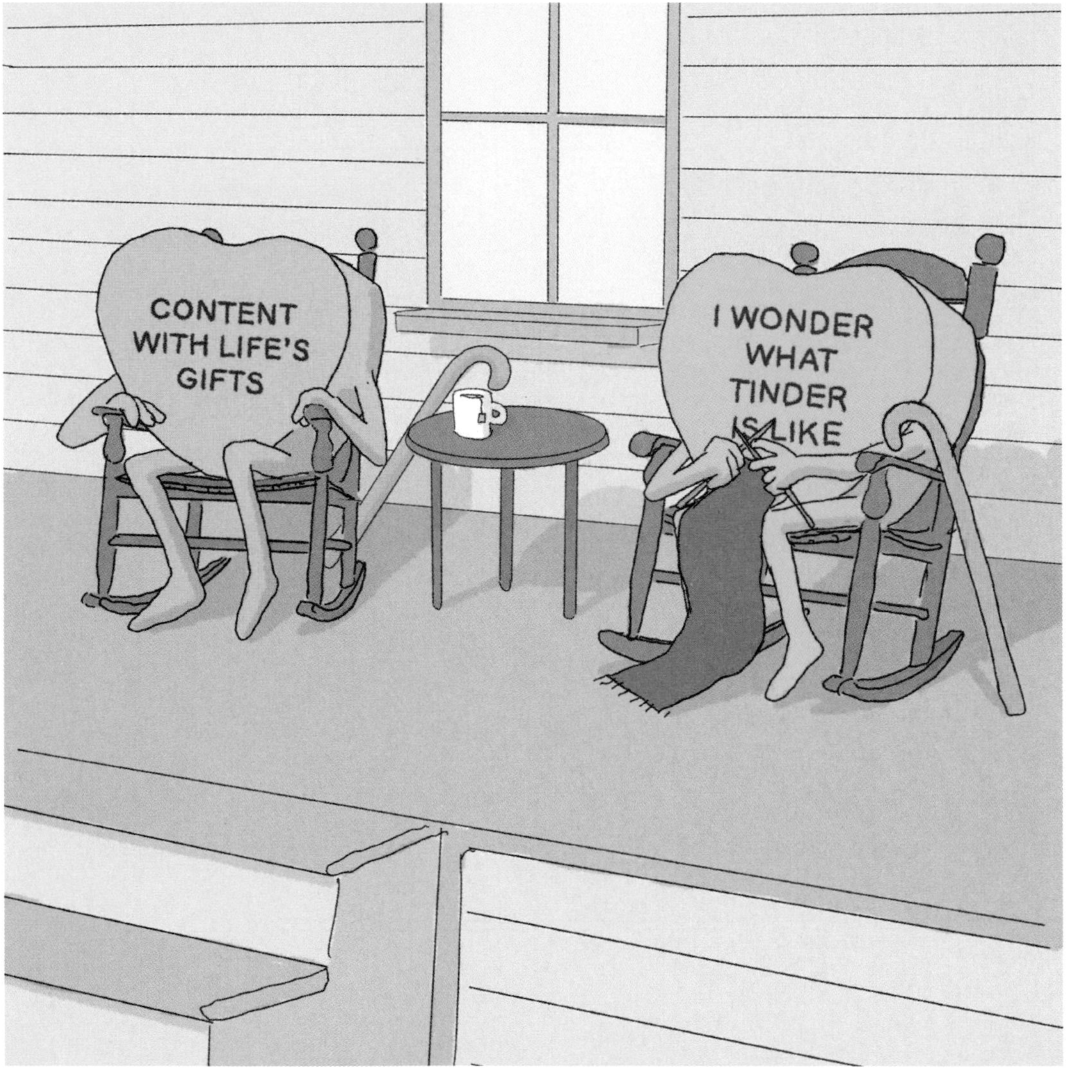
CONTENT WITH LIFE'S GIFTS
I WONDER WHAT TINDER IS LIKE

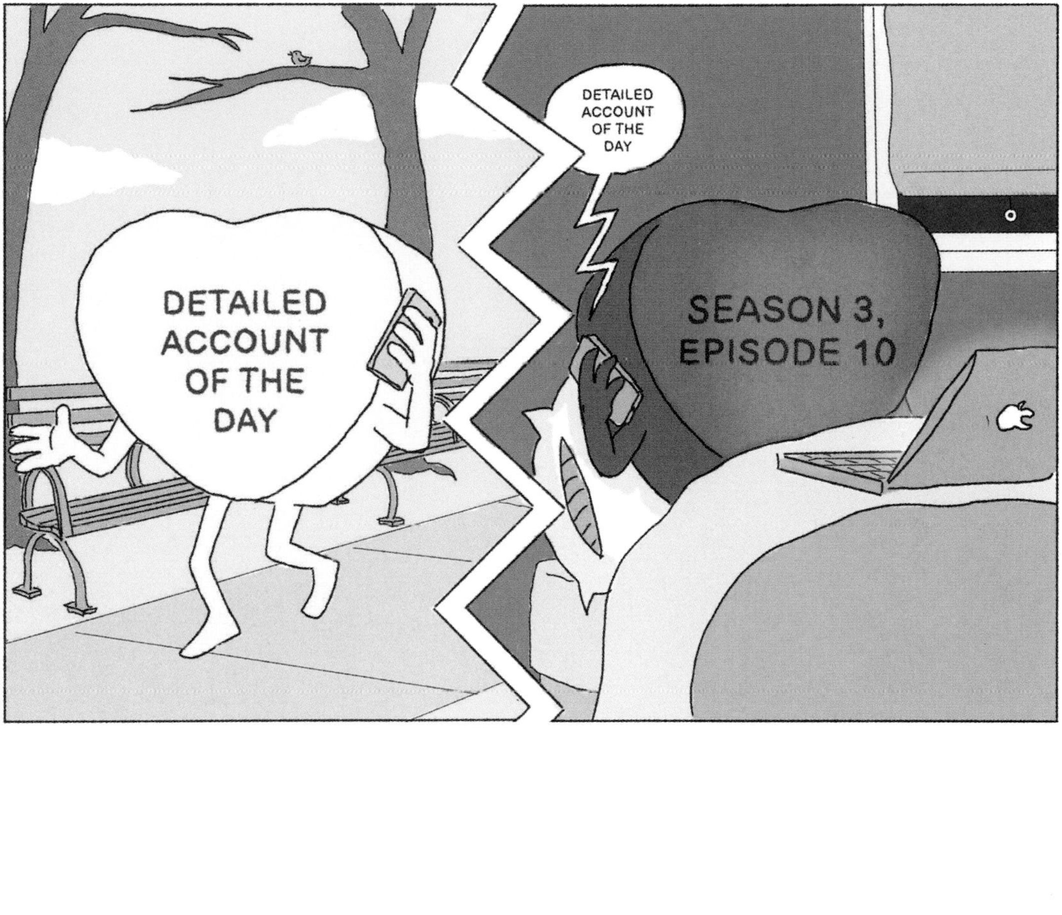
DETAILED ACCOUNT OF THE DAY
DETAILED ACCOUNT OF THE DAY
SEASON 3, EPISODE 10

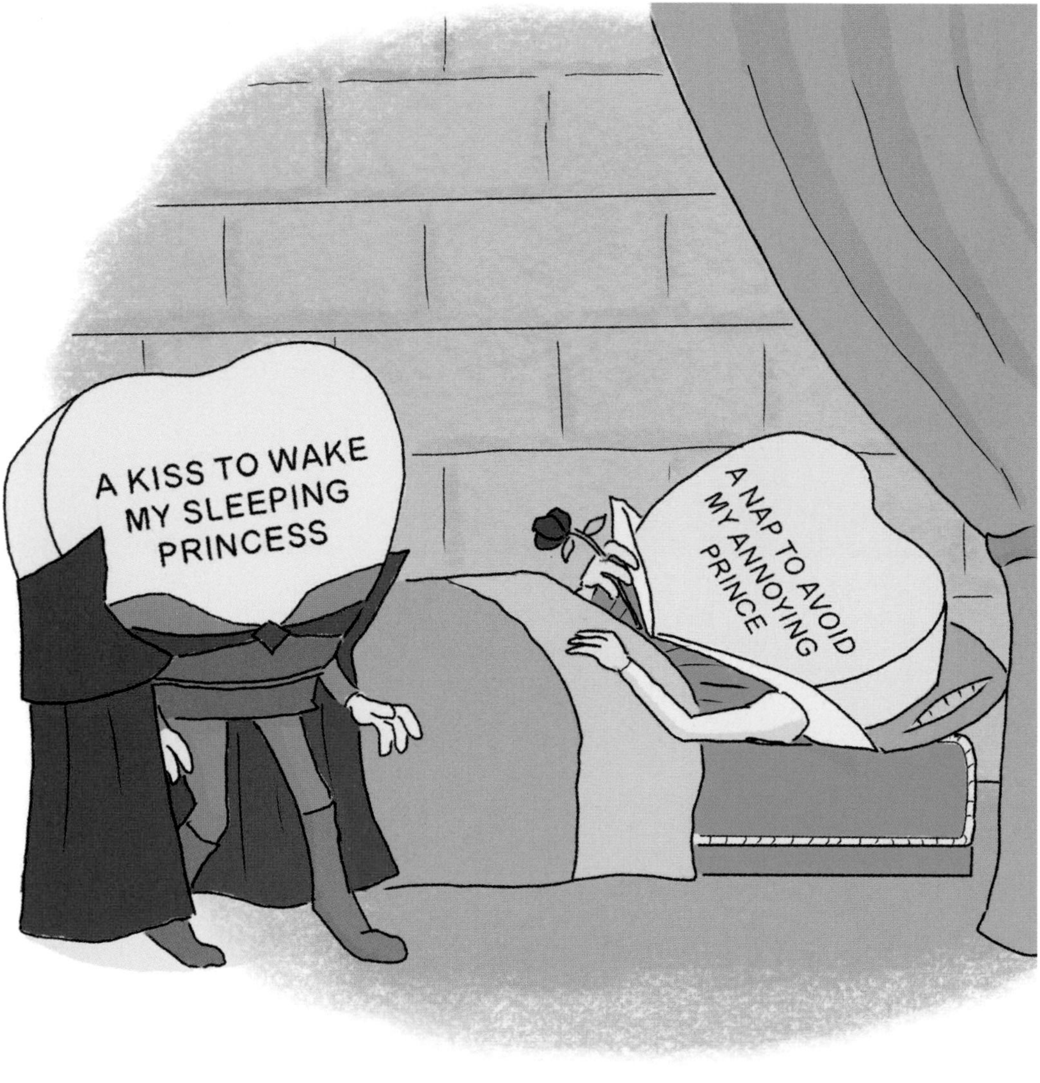
A KISS TO WAKE
MY SLEEPING
PRINCESS
A NAP TO AVOID
MY ANNOYING
PRINCE

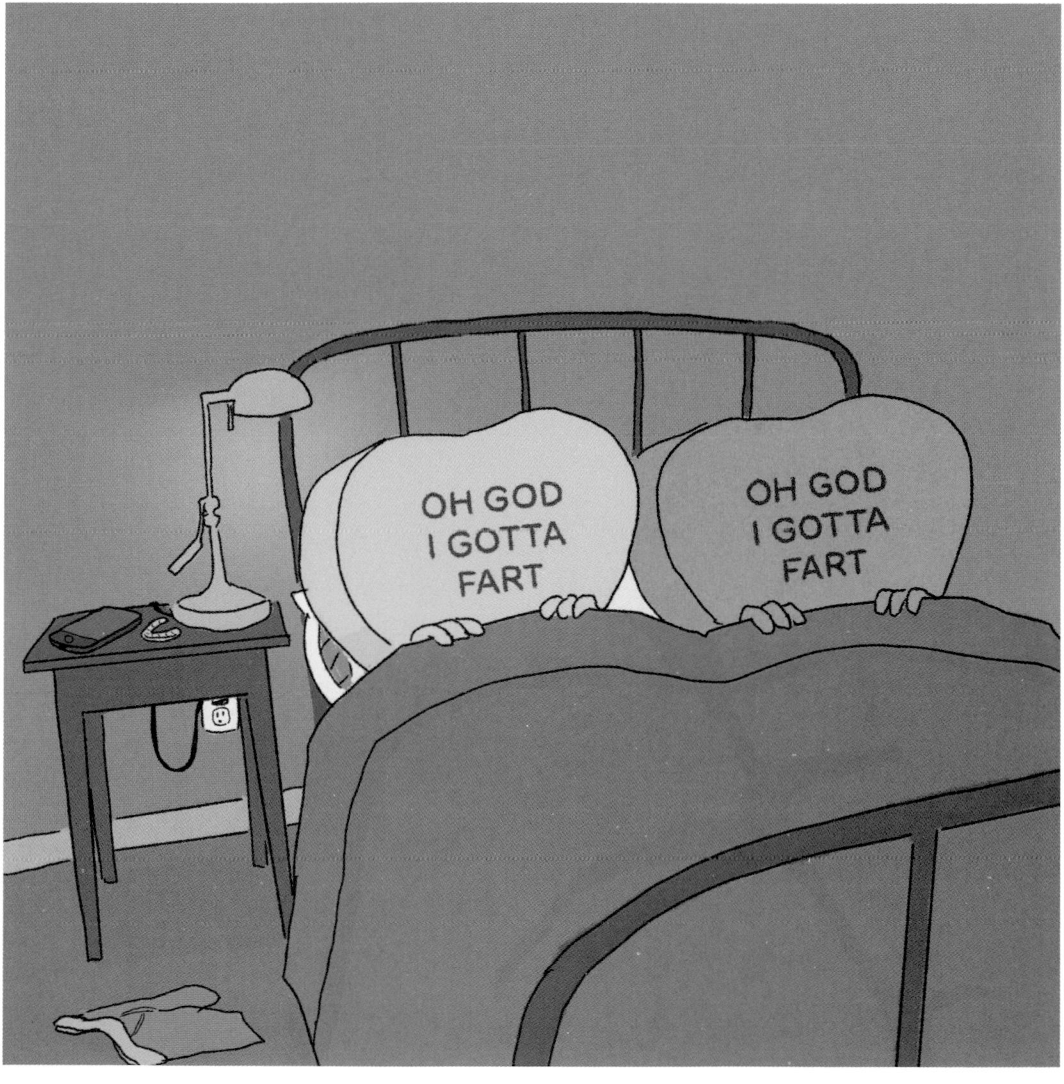
OH GOD
I GOTTA
FART
OH GOD
I GOTTA
FART

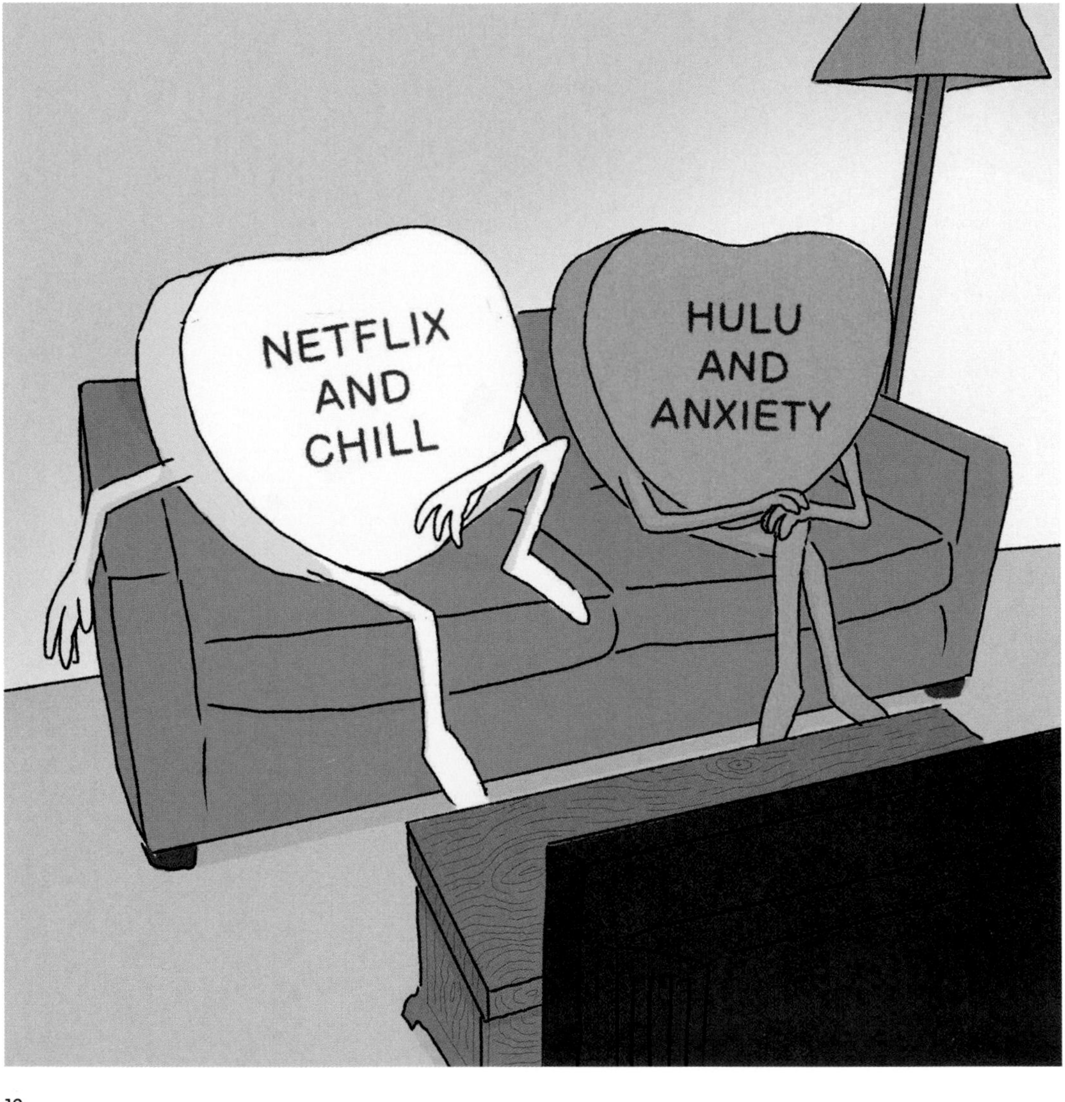
NETFLIX
AND
CHILL
HULU
AND
ANXIETY

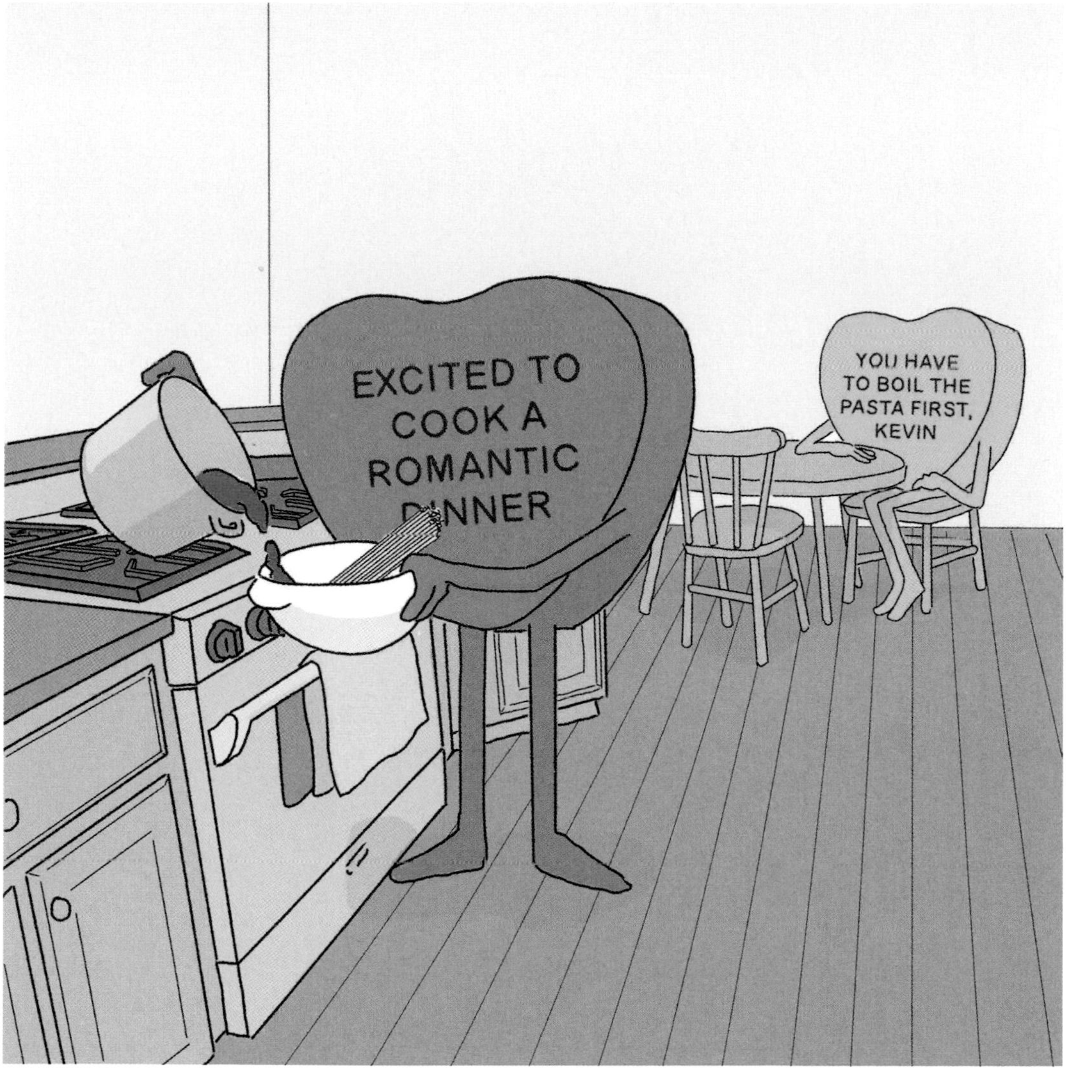
EXCITED TO COOK A ROMANTIC DINNER
YOU HAVE TO BOIL THE PASTA FIRST, KEVIN

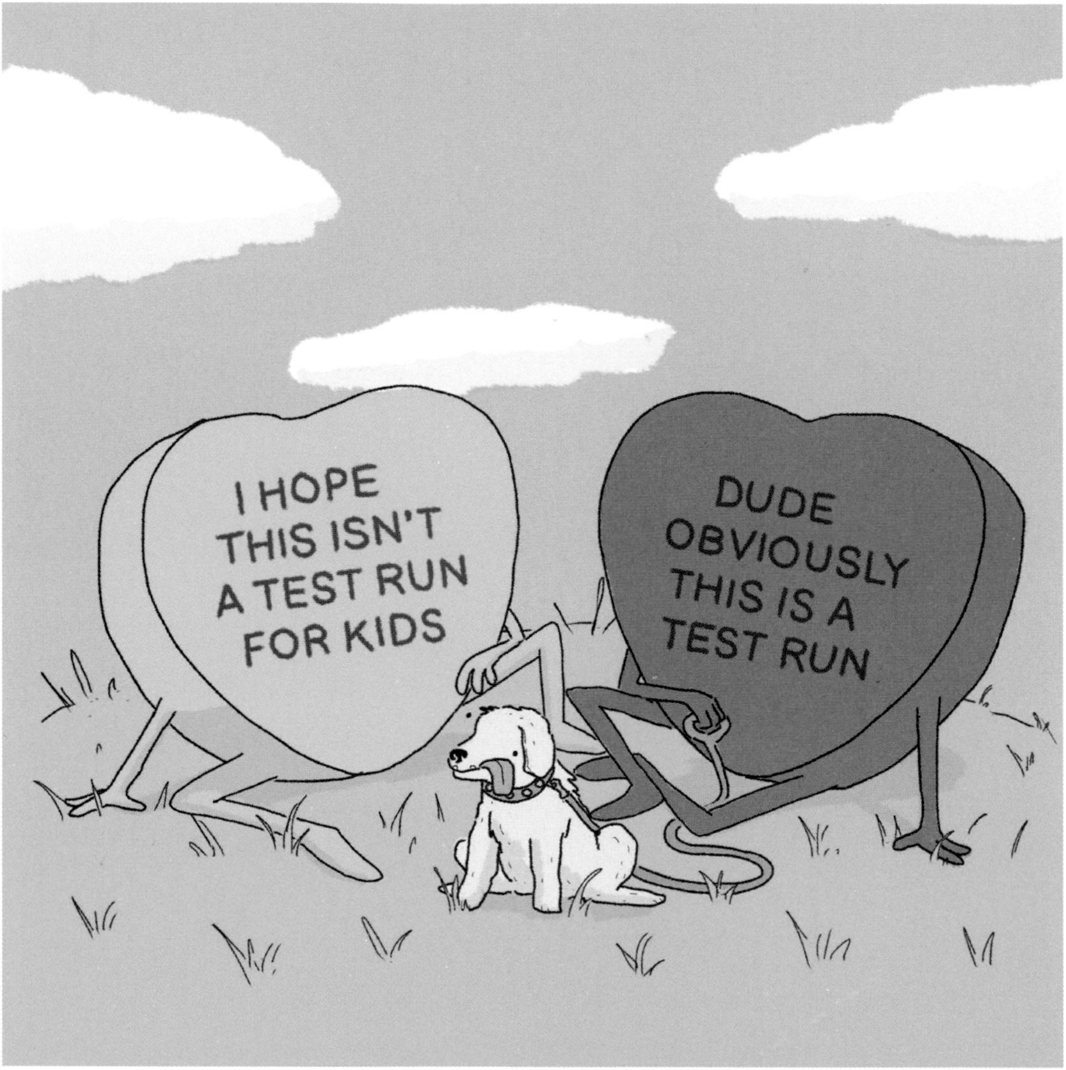
I HOPE THIS ISN'T A TEST RUN FOR KIDS
DUDE OBVIOUSLY THIS IS A TEST RUN

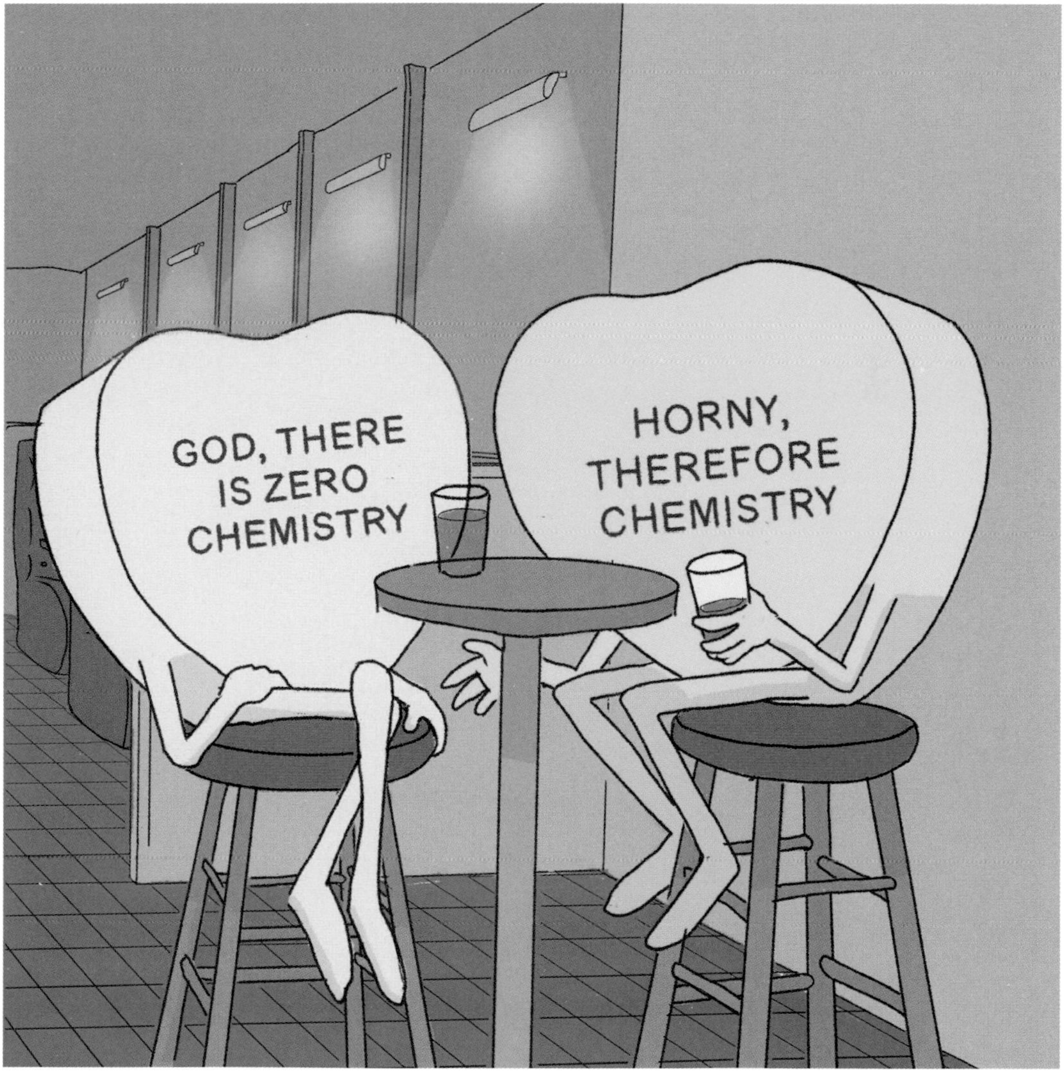
GOD, THERE IS ZERO CHEMISTRY
HORNY, THEREFORE CHEMISTRY

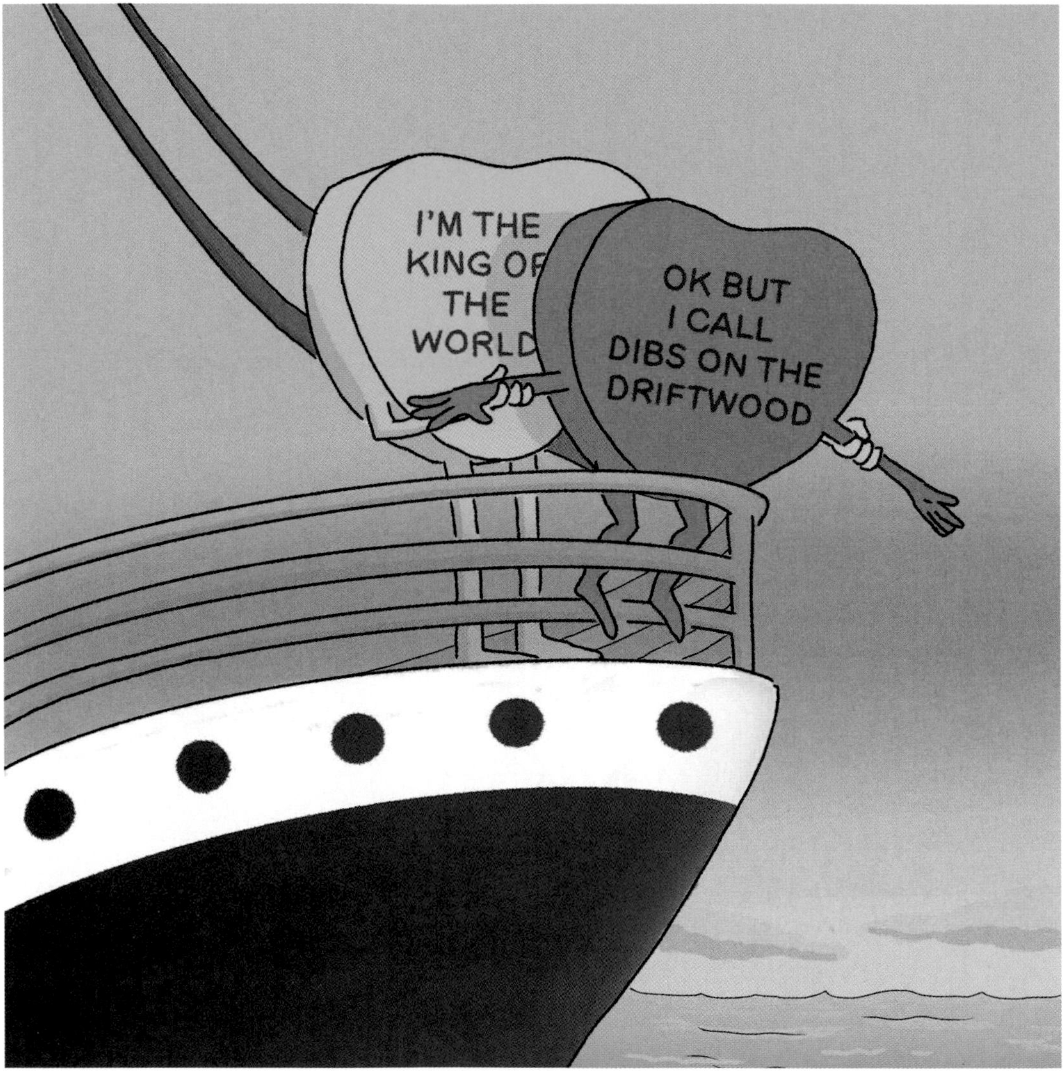
I'M THE
KING OF
THE
WORLD
OK BUT
I CALL
DIBS ON THE
DRIFTWOOD

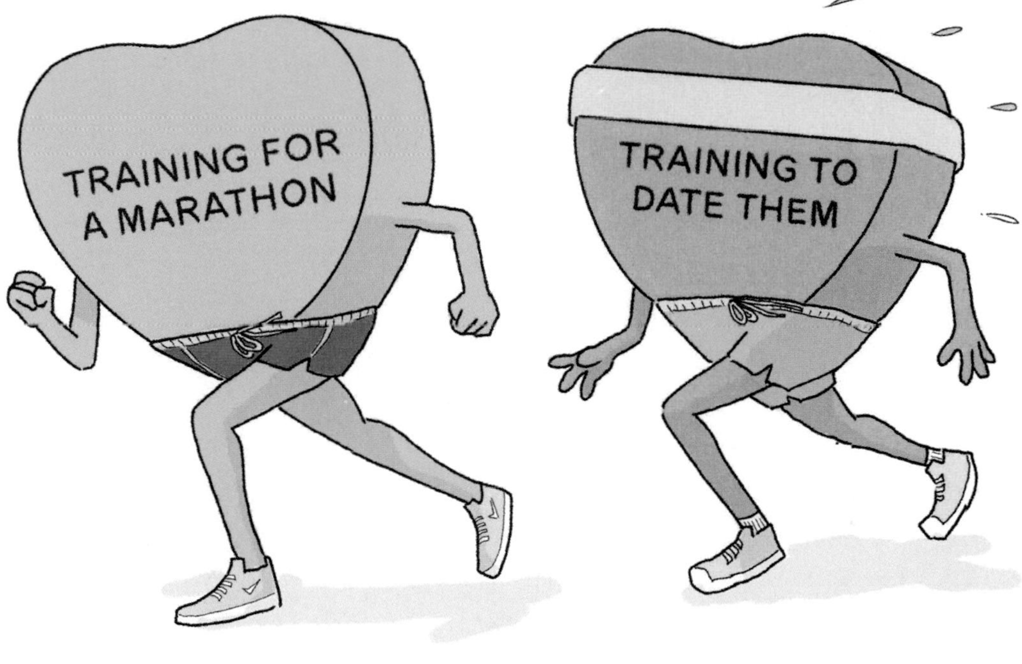
TRAINING FOR
A MARATHON
TRAINING TO
DATE THEM

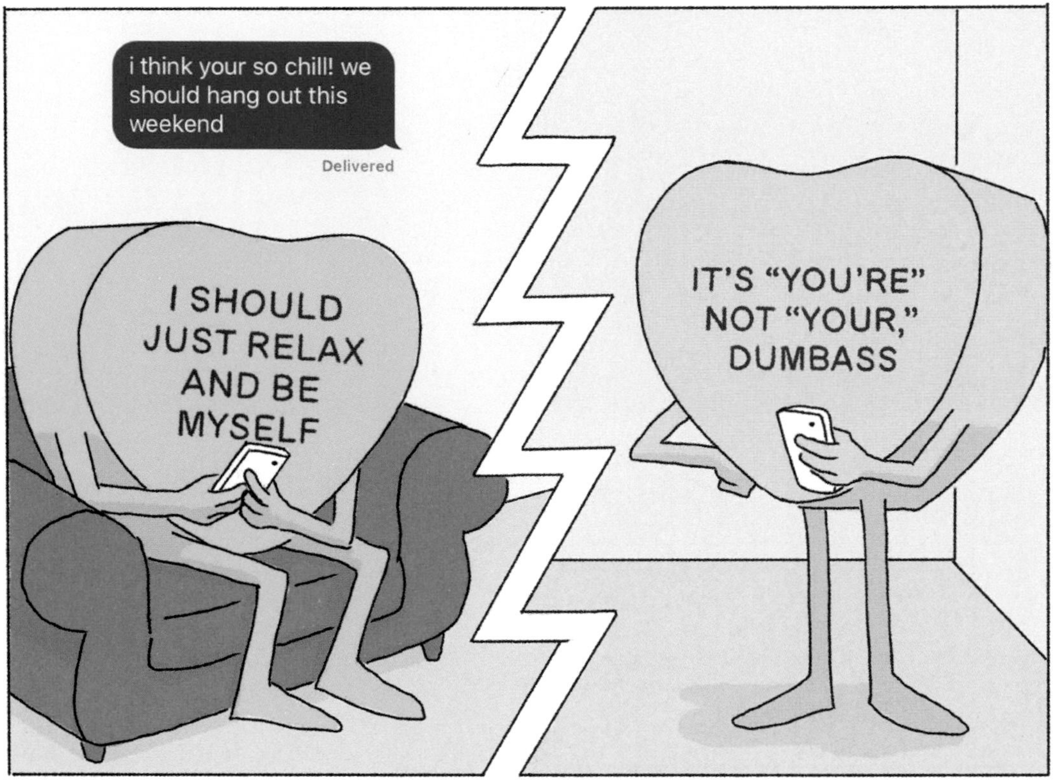
i think your so chill! we should hang out this weekend
Delivered
I SHOULD JUST RELAX AND BE MYSELF
IT'S "YOU'RE" NOT "YOUR," DUMBASS

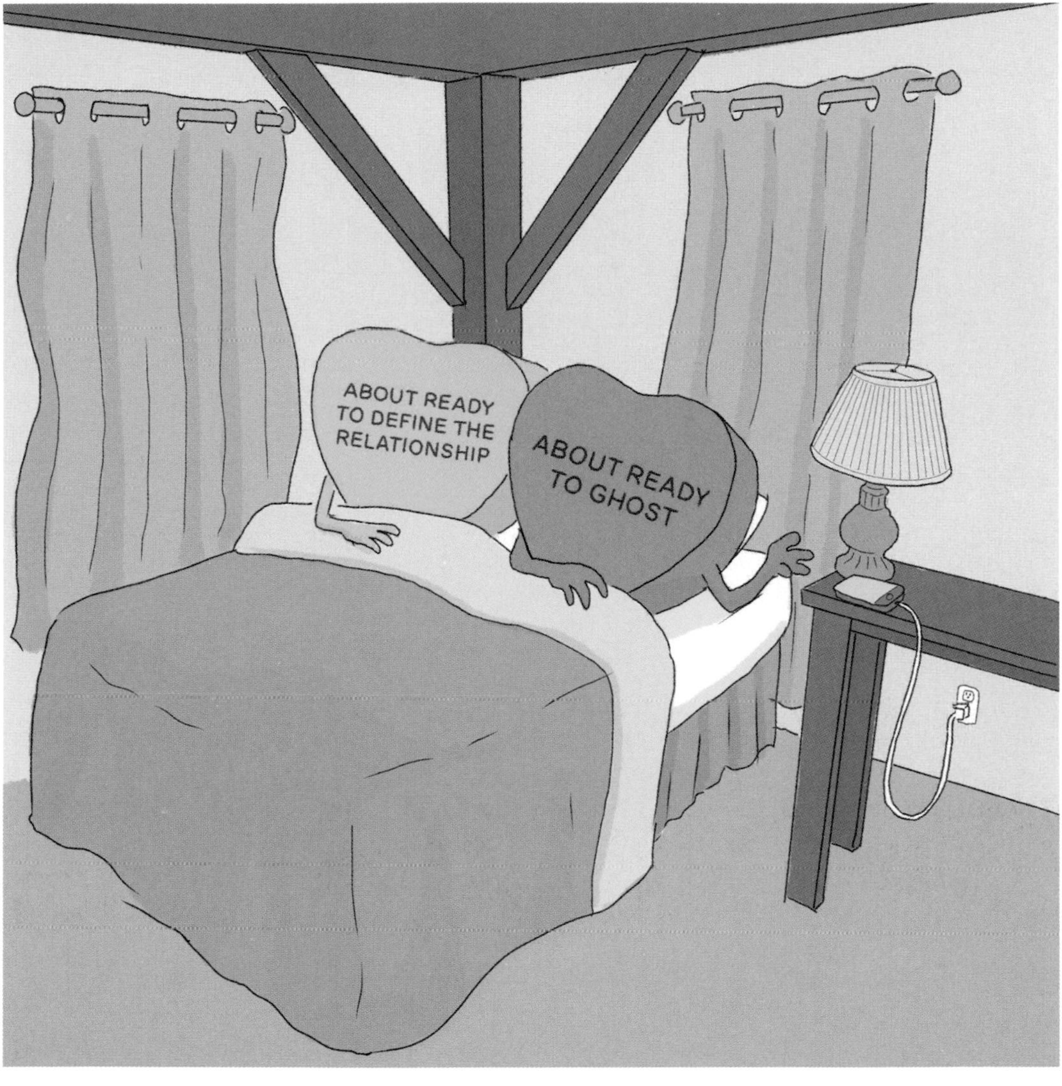
ABOUT READY TO DEFINE THE RELATIONSHIP
ABOUT READY TO GHOST

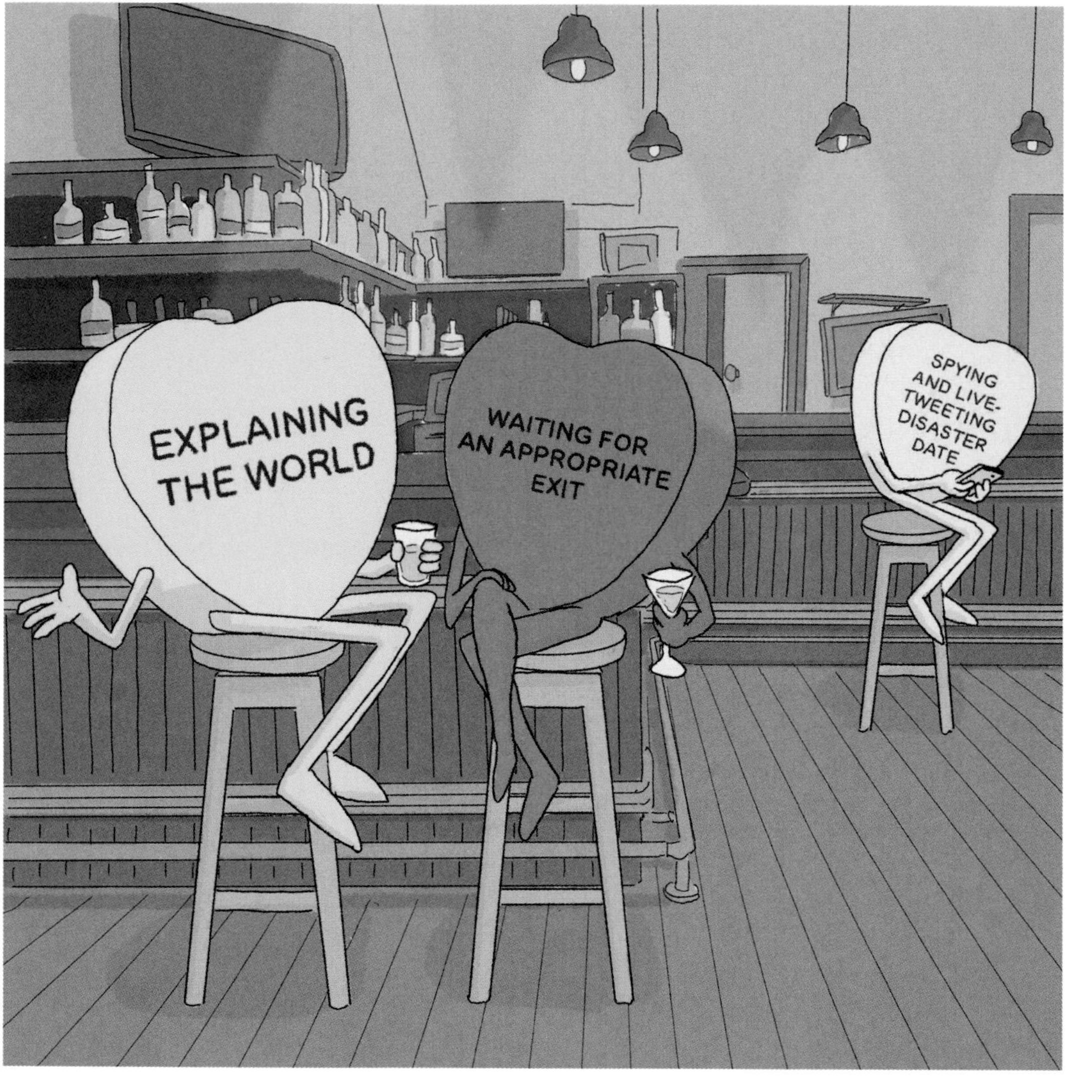
EXPLAINING
THE WORLD
WAITING FOR
AN APPROPRIATE
EXIT
SPYING
AND LIVE-
TWEETING
DISASTER
DATE

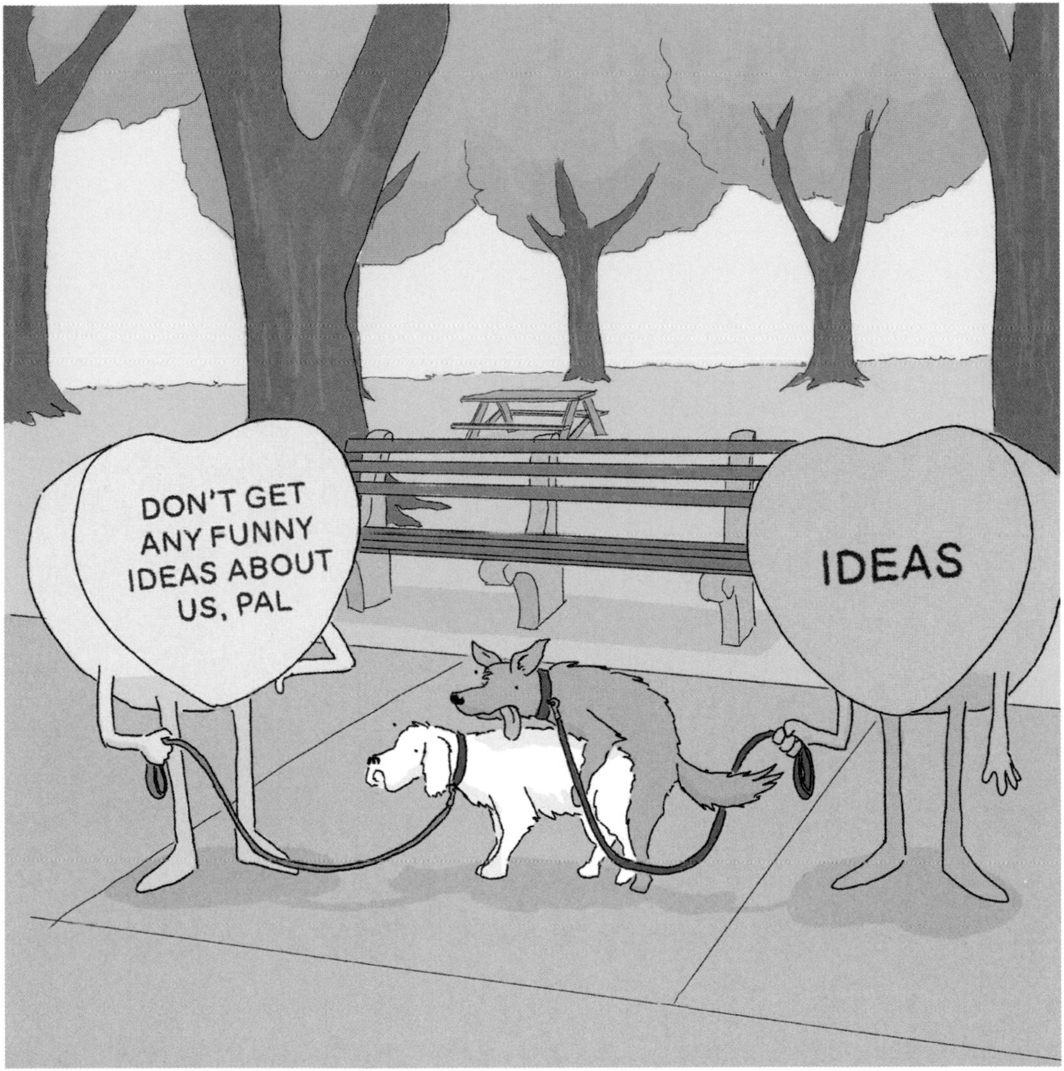
DON'T GET ANY FUNNY IDEAS ABOUT US, PAL
IDEAS

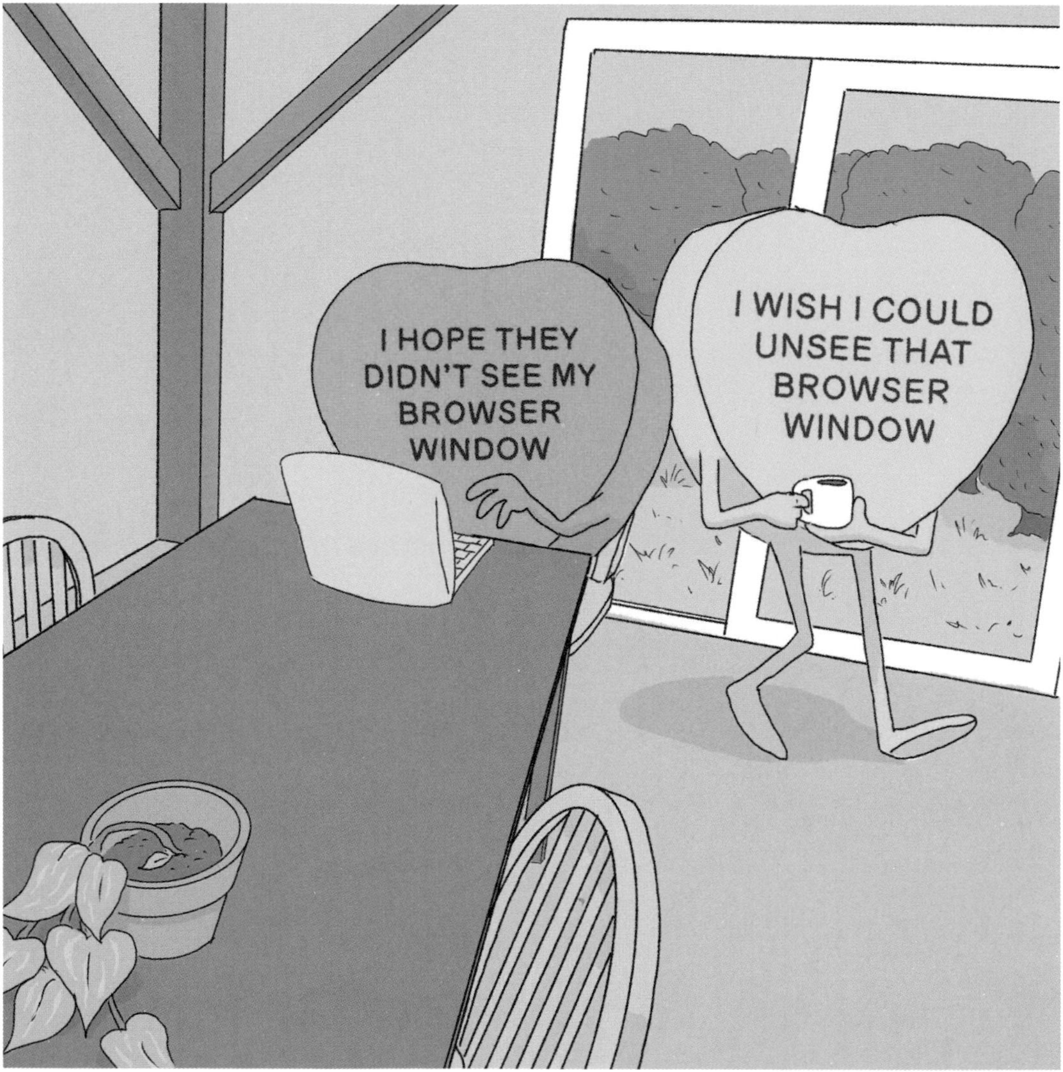
I HOPE THEY DIDN'T SEE MY BROWSER WINDOW
I WISH I COULD UNSEE THAT BROWSER WINDOW

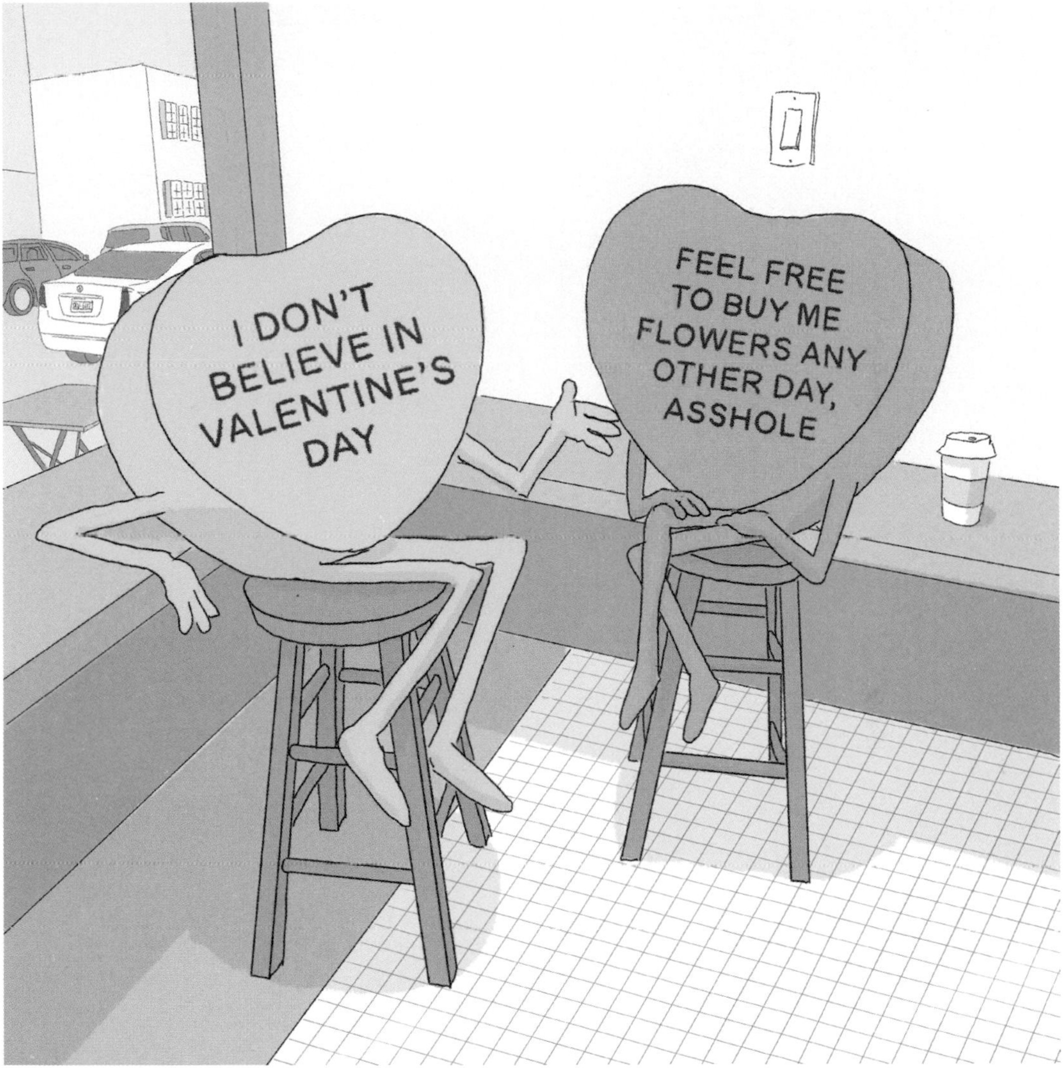
I DON'T BELIEVE IN VALENTINE'S DAY
FEEL FREE TO BUY ME FLOWERS ANY OTHER DAY, ASSHOLE

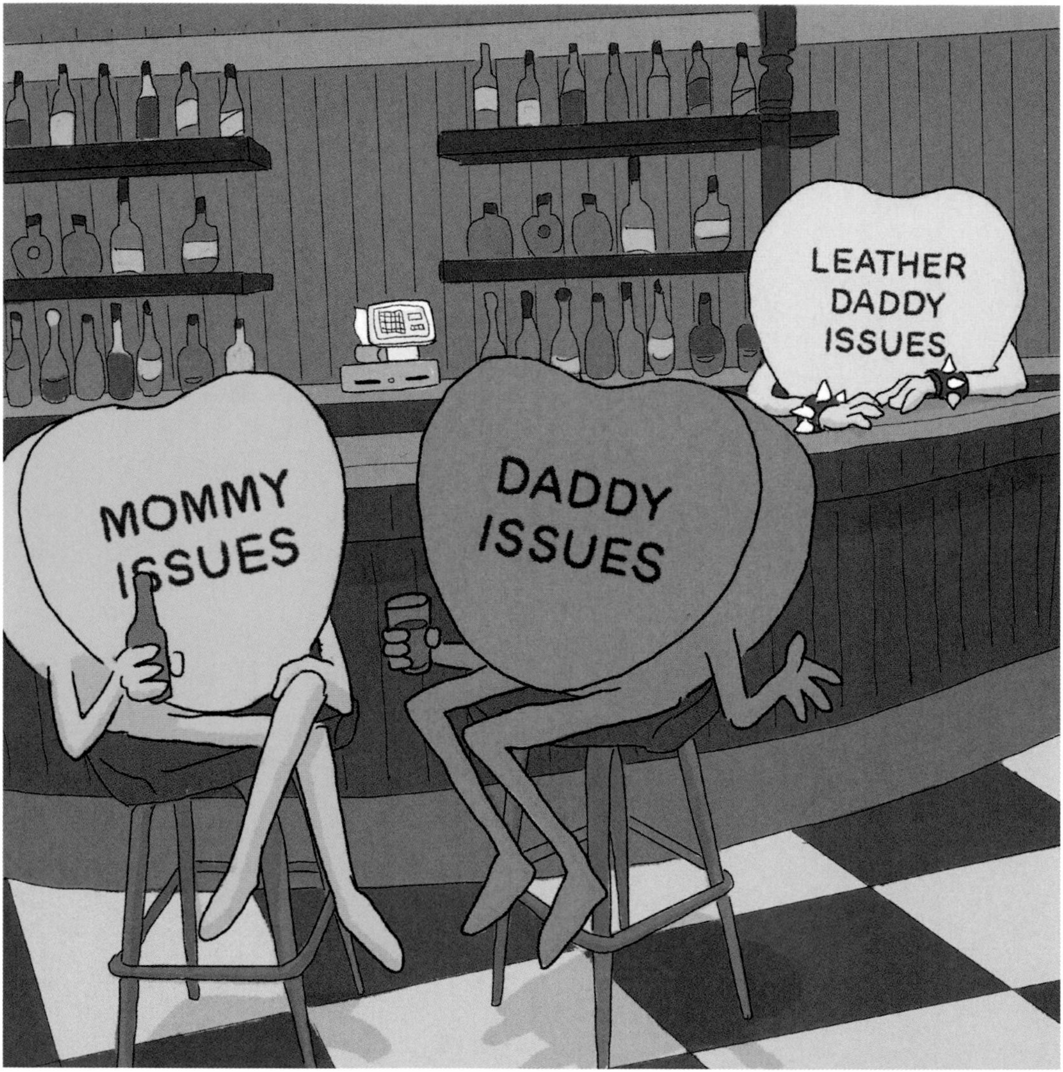
LEATHER
DADDY
ISSUES
MOMMY
ISSUES
DADDY
ISSUES

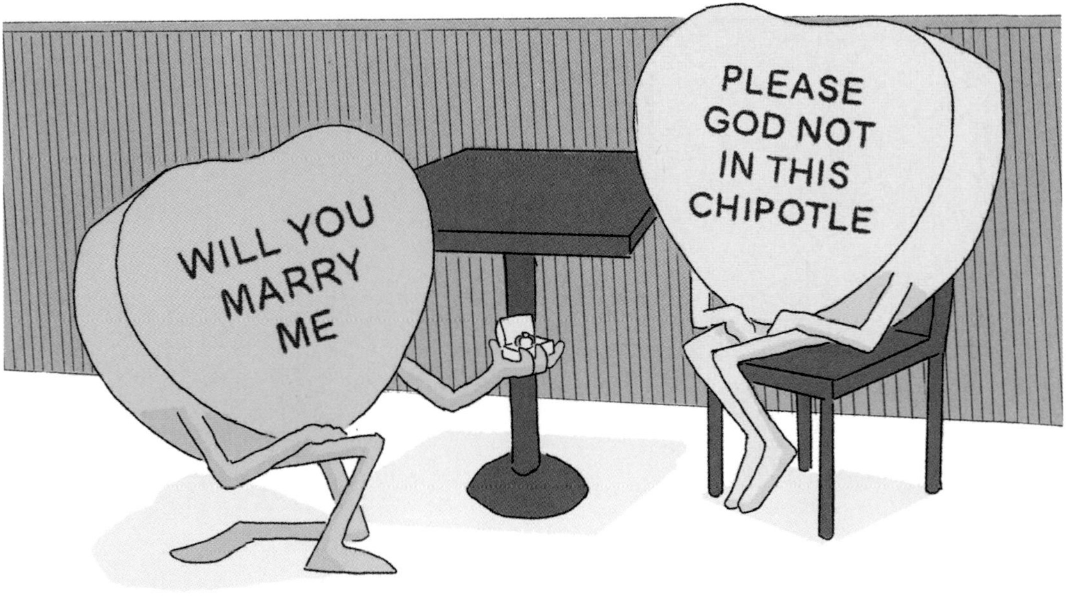
WILL YOU
MARRY
ME
PLEASE
GOD NOT
IN THIS
CHIPOTLE

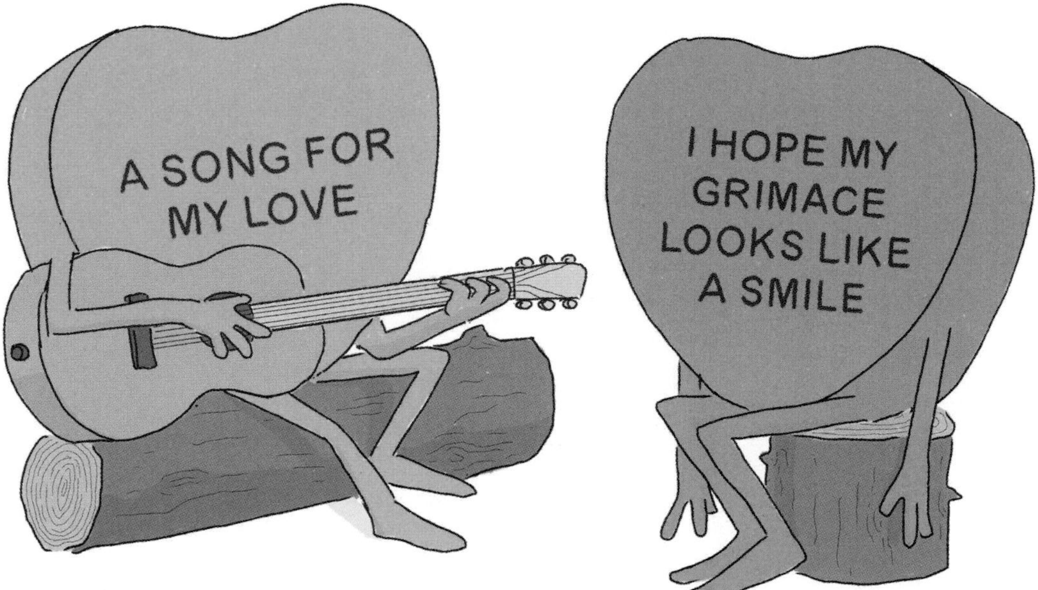
A SONG FOR
MY LOVE
I HOPE MY
GRIMACE
LOOKS LIKE
A SMILE

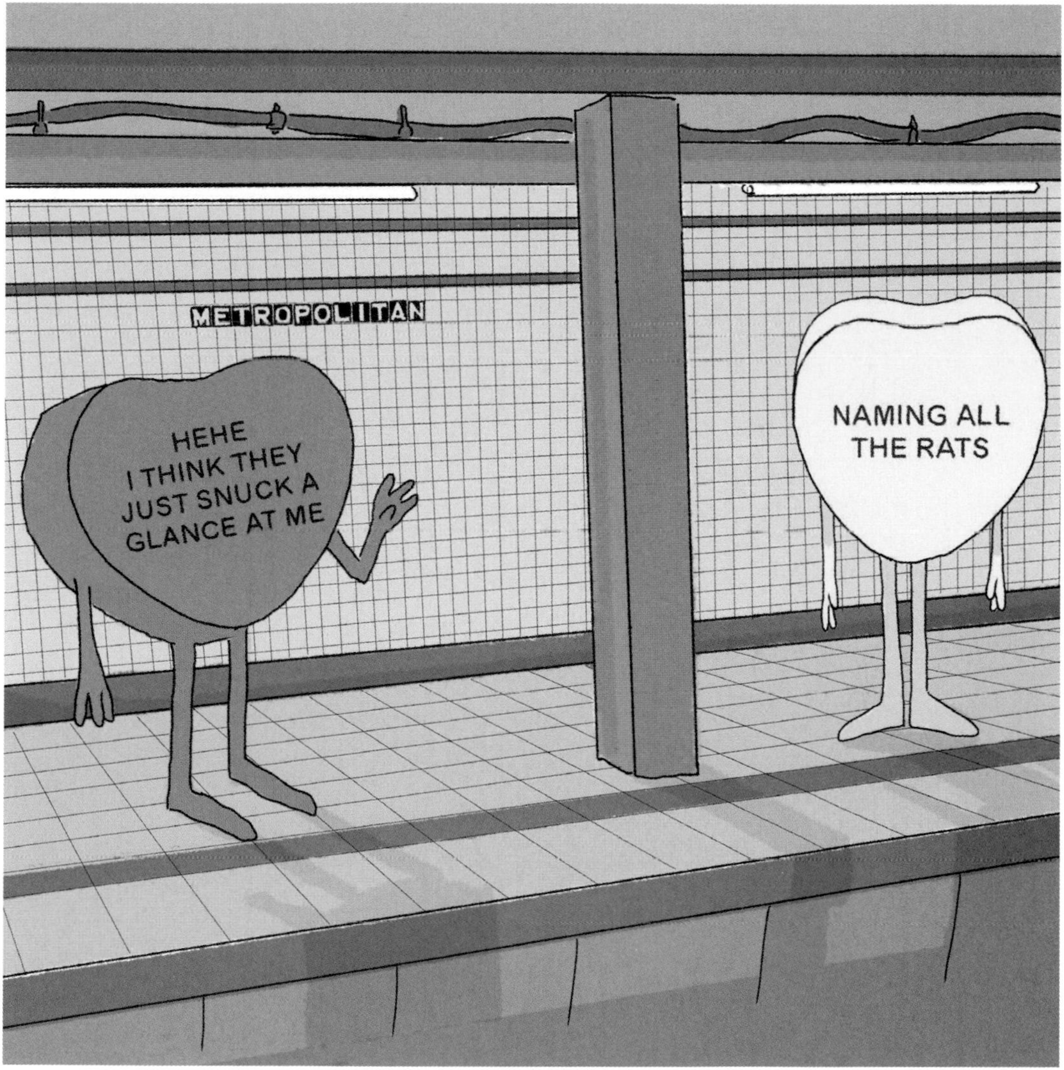
METROPOLITAN
HEHE I THINK THEY JUST SNUCK A GLANCE AT ME
NAMING ALL THE RATS

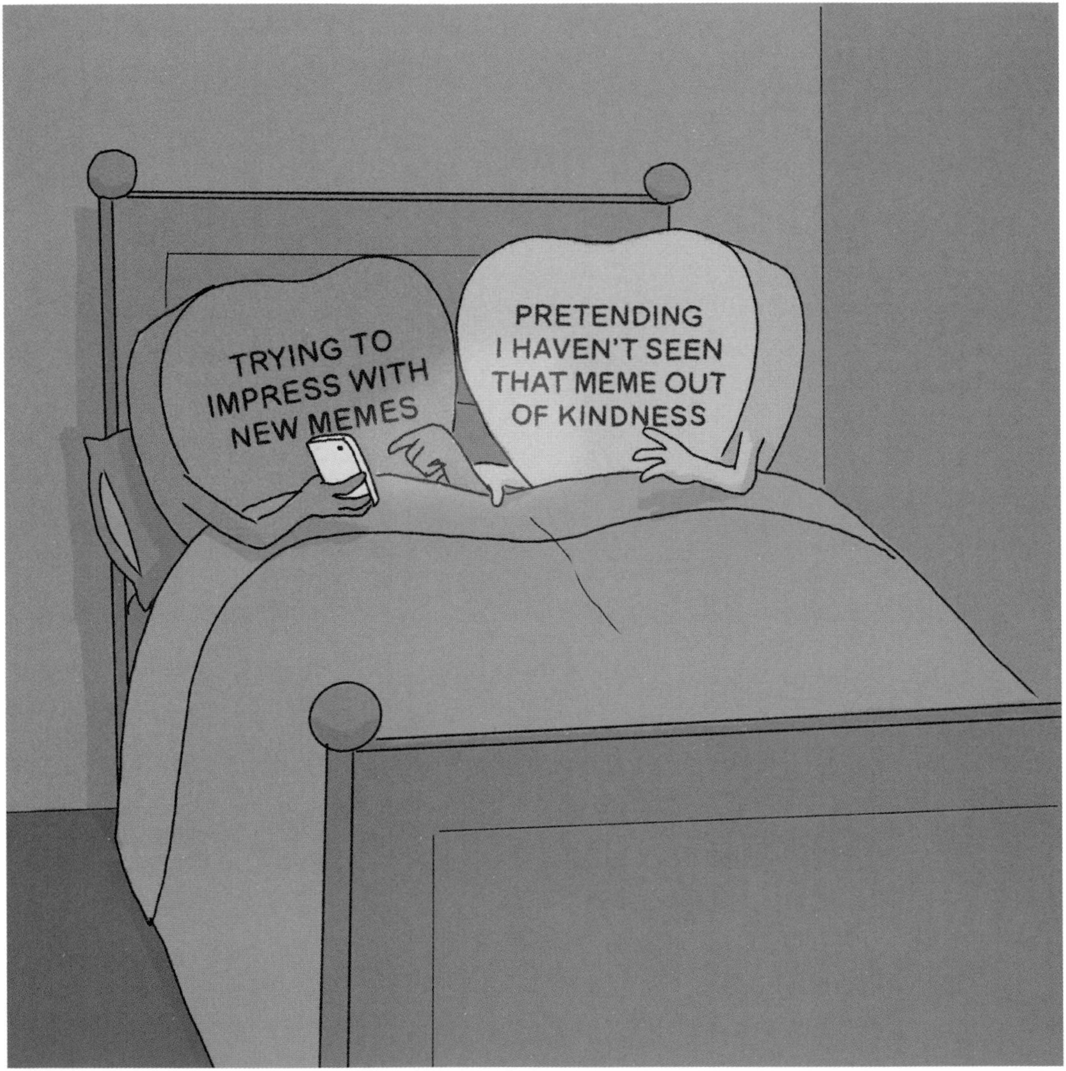
TRYING TO IMPRESS WITH NEW MEMES
PRETENDING I HAVEN'T SEEN THAT MEME OUT OF KINDNESS

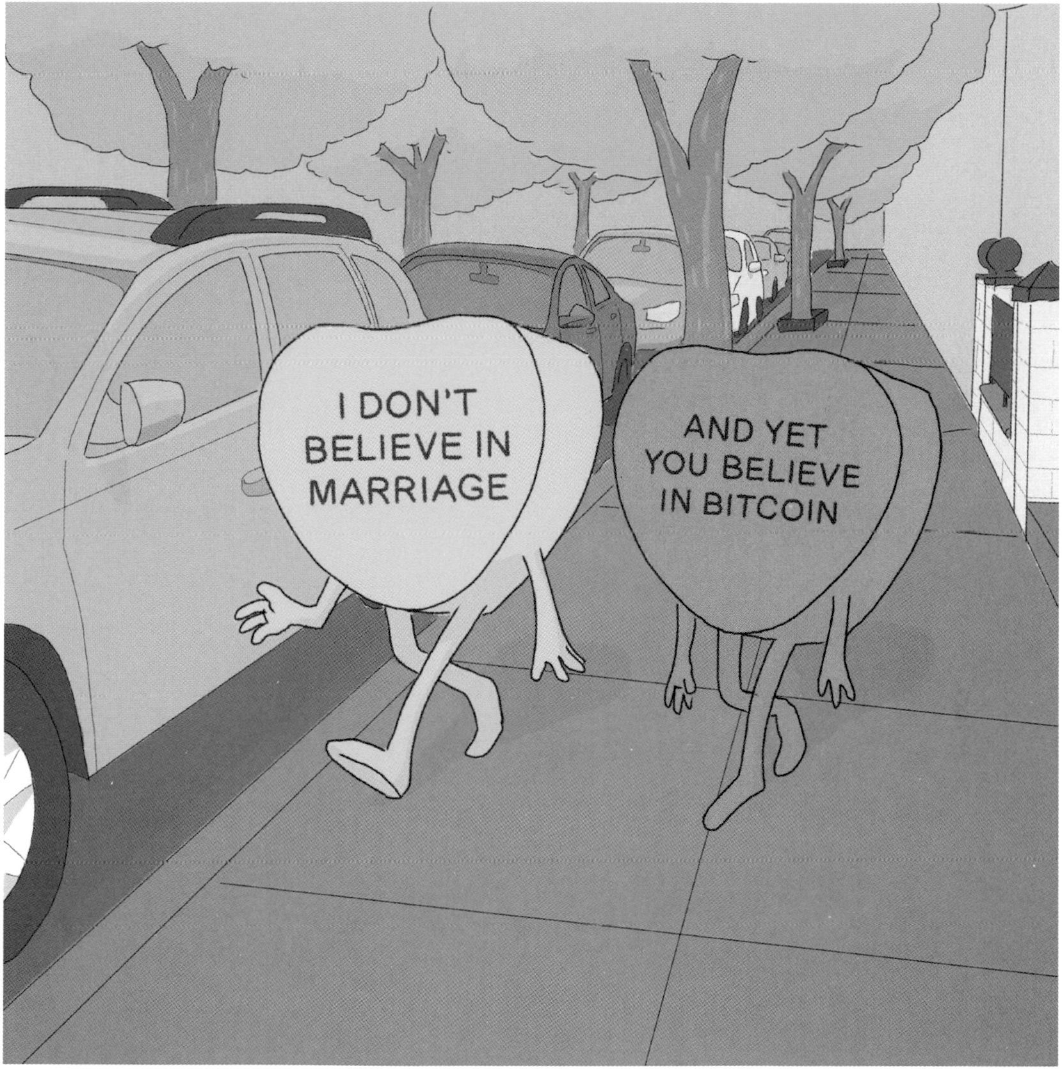
I DON'T BELIEVE IN MARRIAGE
AND YET YOU BELIEVE IN BITCOIN

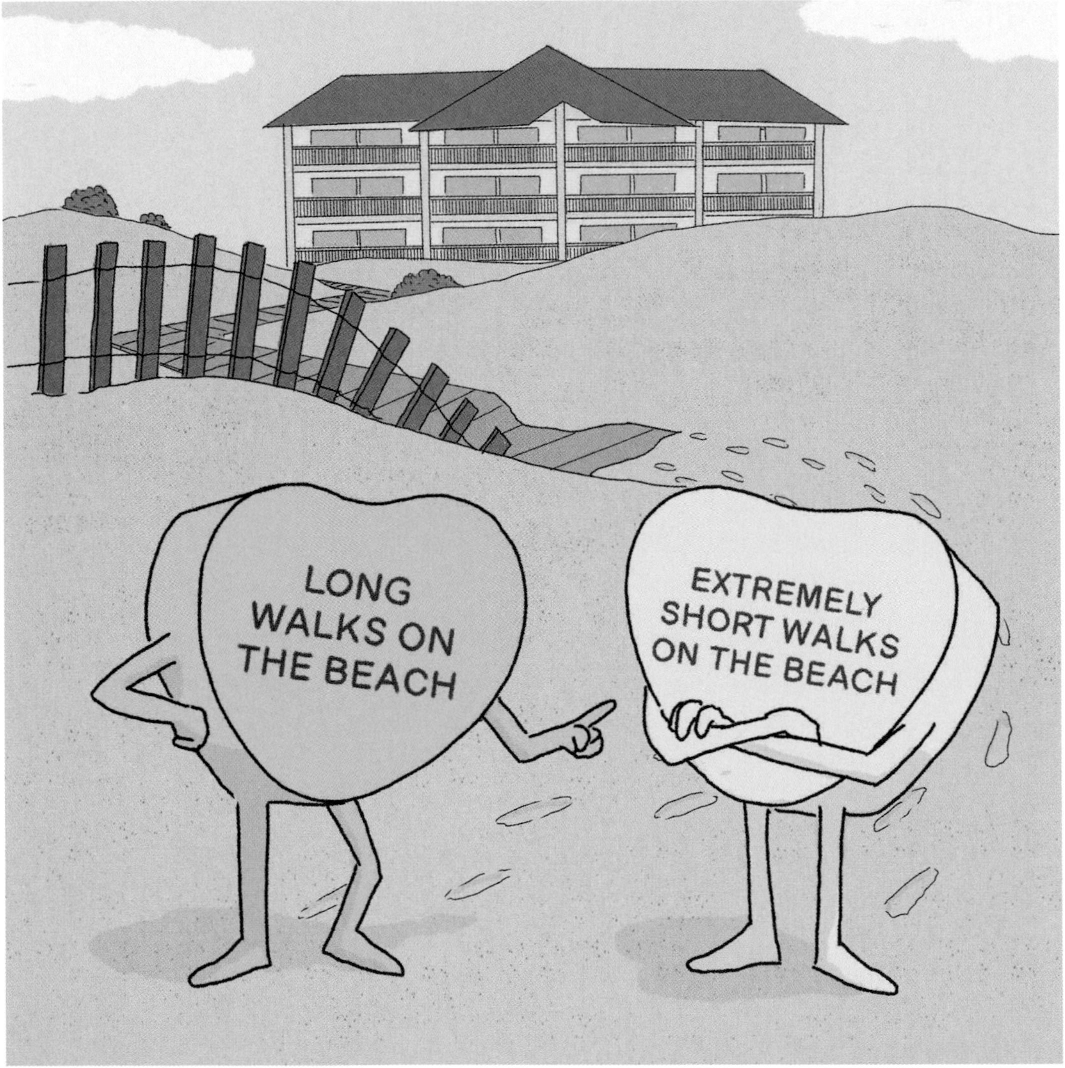
LONG
WALKS ON
THE BEACH
EXTREMELY
SHORT WALKS
ON THE BEACH

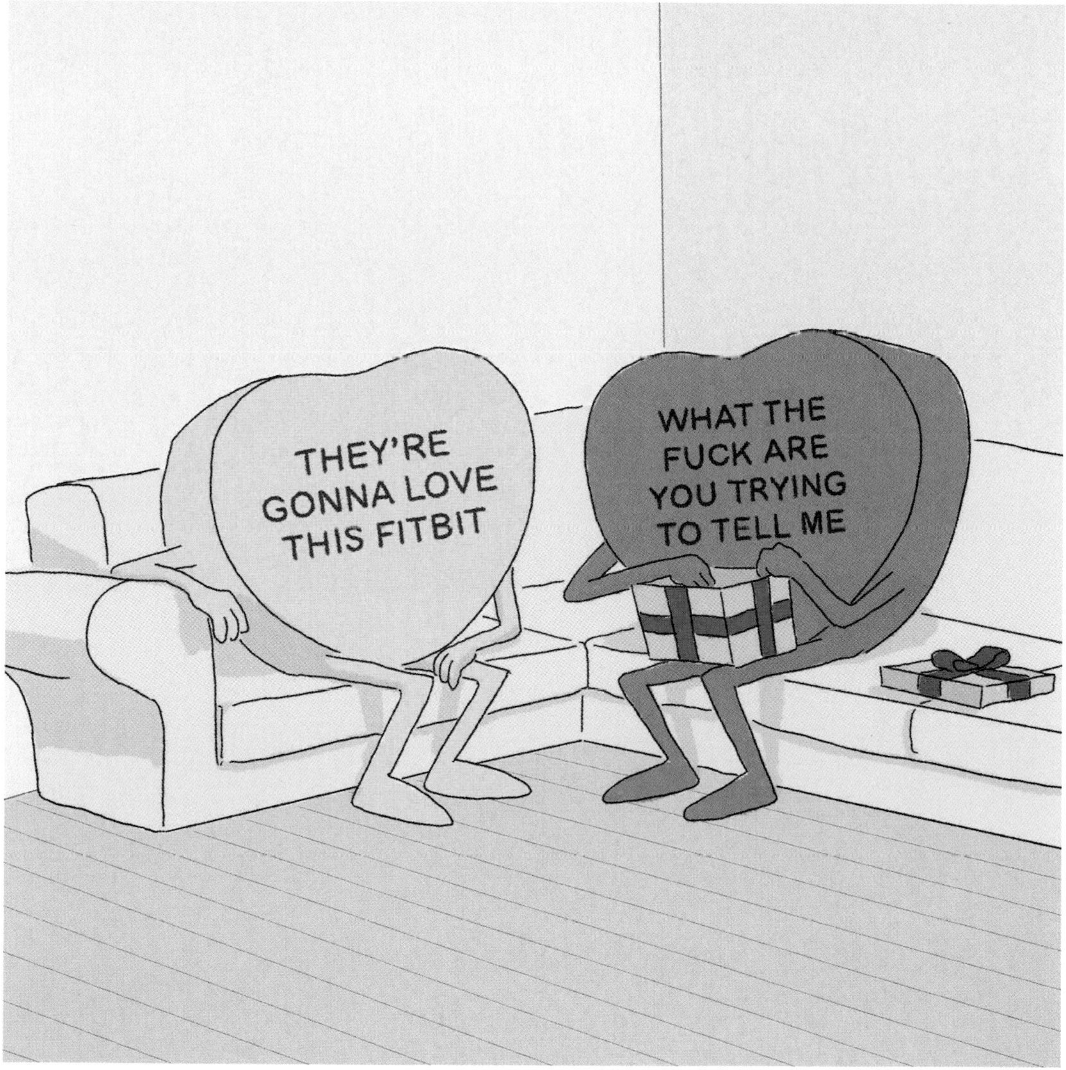
THEY'RE GONNA LOVE THIS FITBIT
WHAT THE FUCK ARE YOU TRYING TO TELL ME

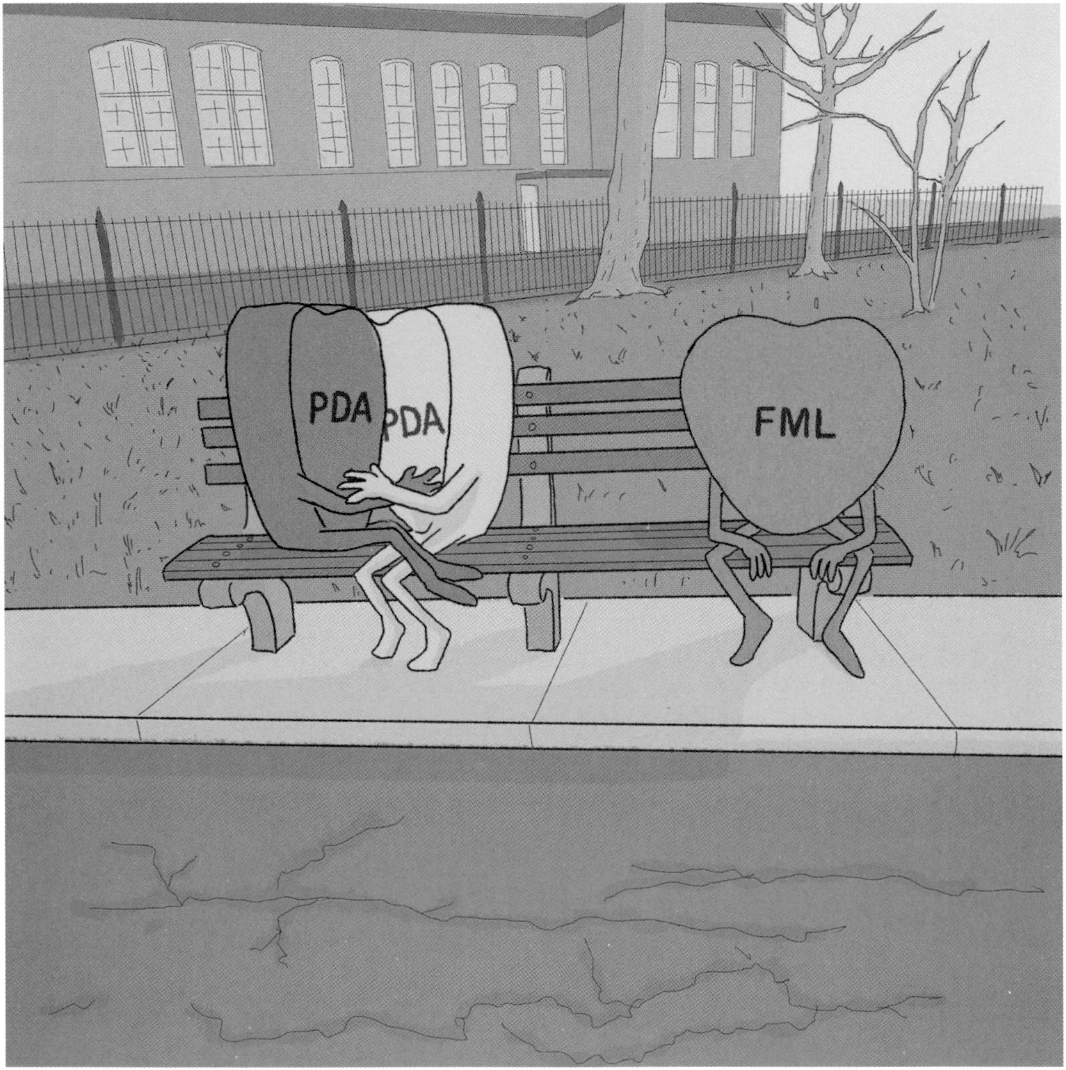
PDA
PDA
FML

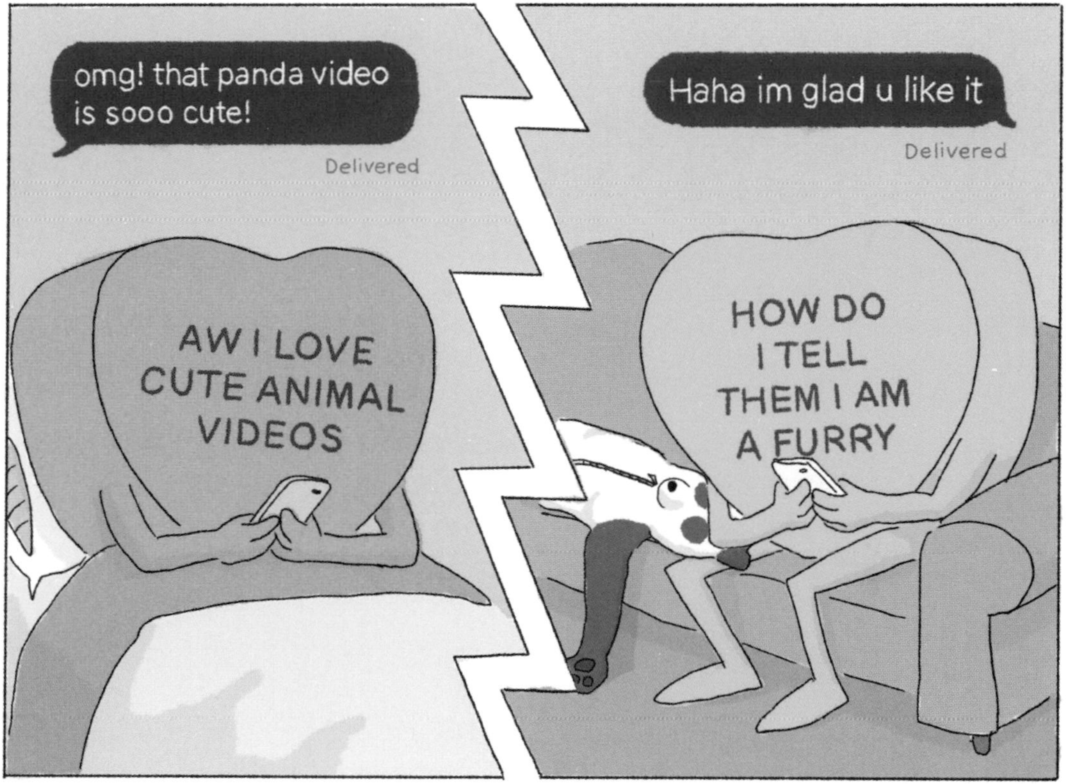
omg! that panda video is sooo cute!
Delivered
AW I LOVE CUTE ANIMAL VIDEOS
Haha im glad u like it
Delivered
HOW DO I TELL THEM I AM A FURRY

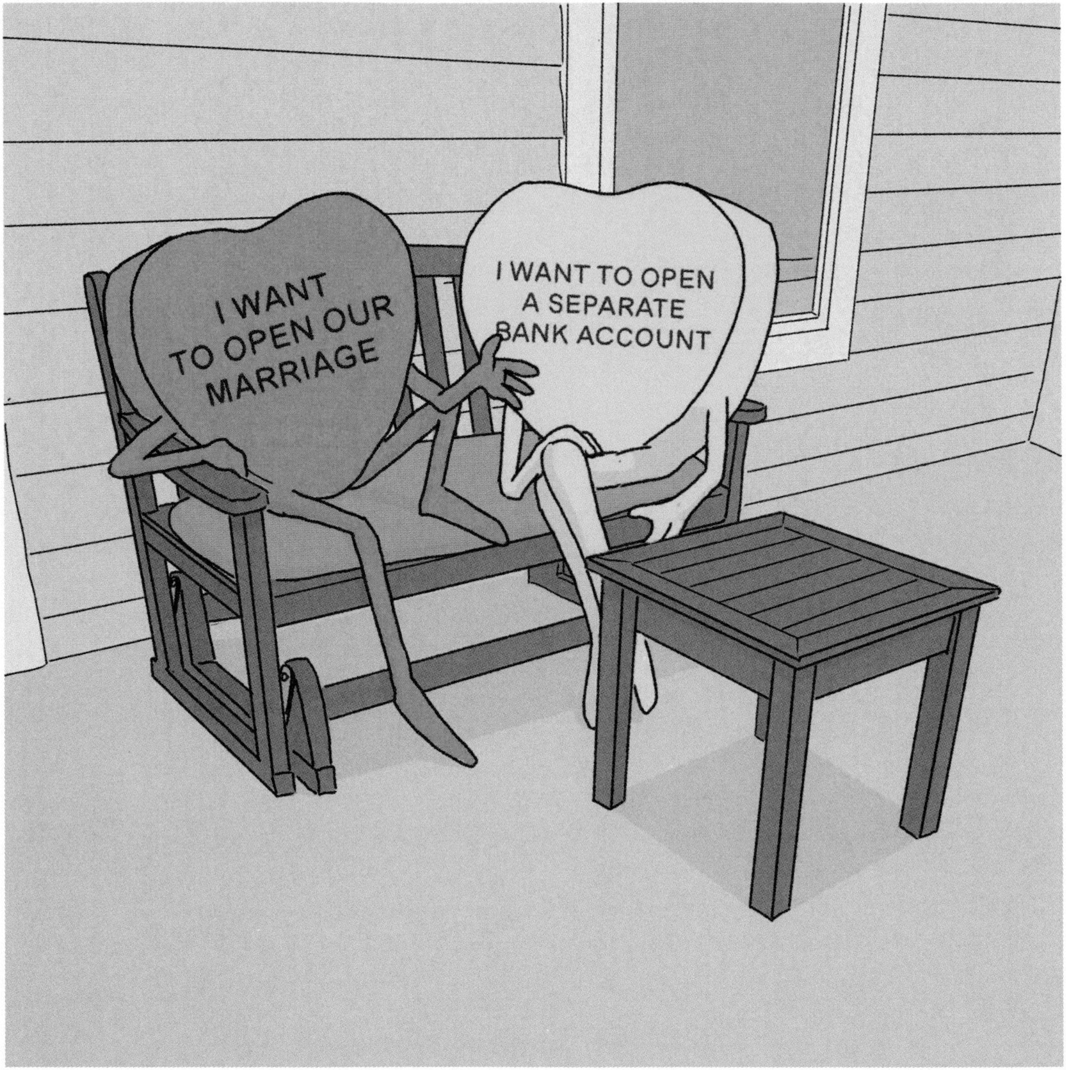
I WANT
TO OPEN OUR
MARRIAGE
I WANT TO OPEN
A SEPARATE
BANK ACCOUNT

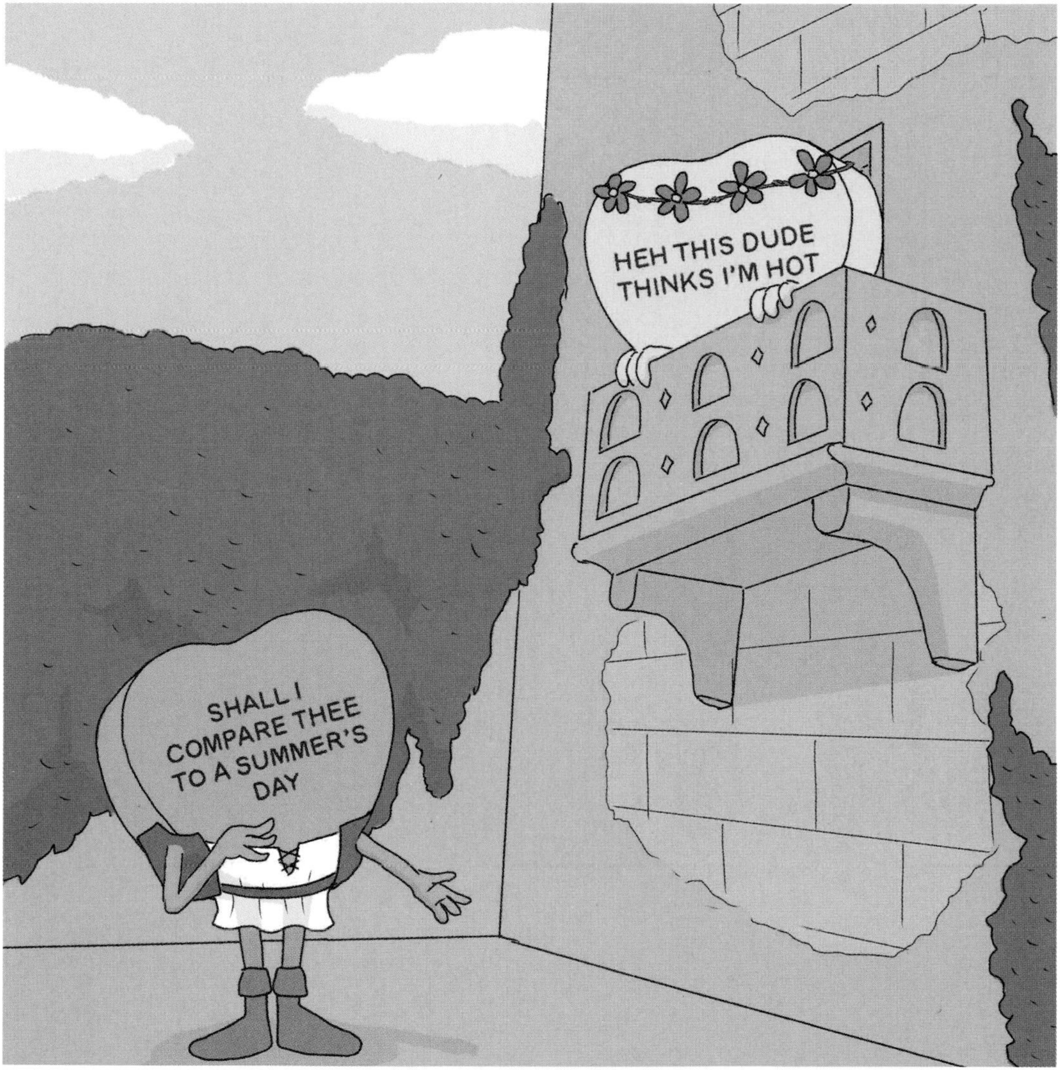
SHALL I COMPARE THEE TO A SUMMER'S DAY
HEH THIS DUDE THINKS I'M HOT

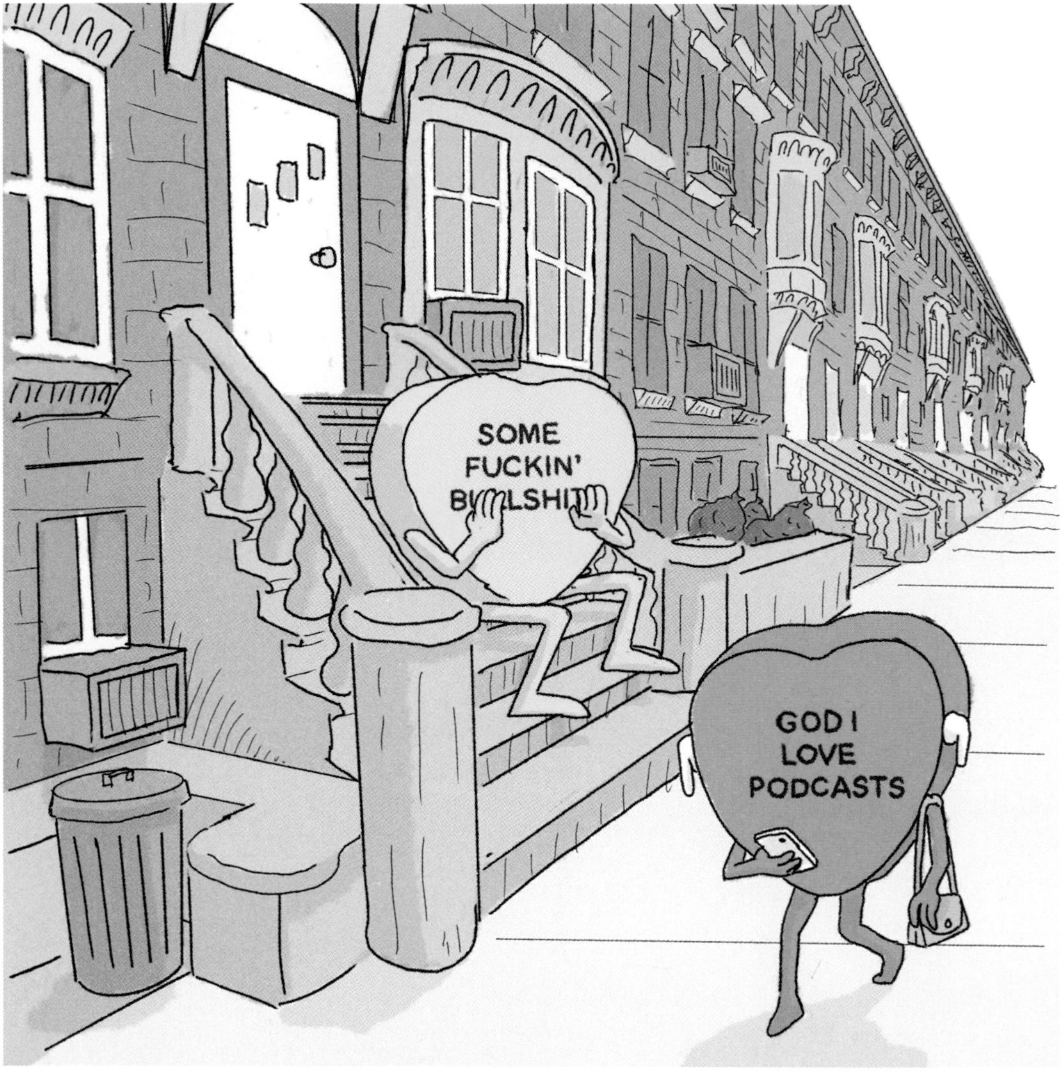
SOME FUCKIN'
GOD I LOVE PODCASTS

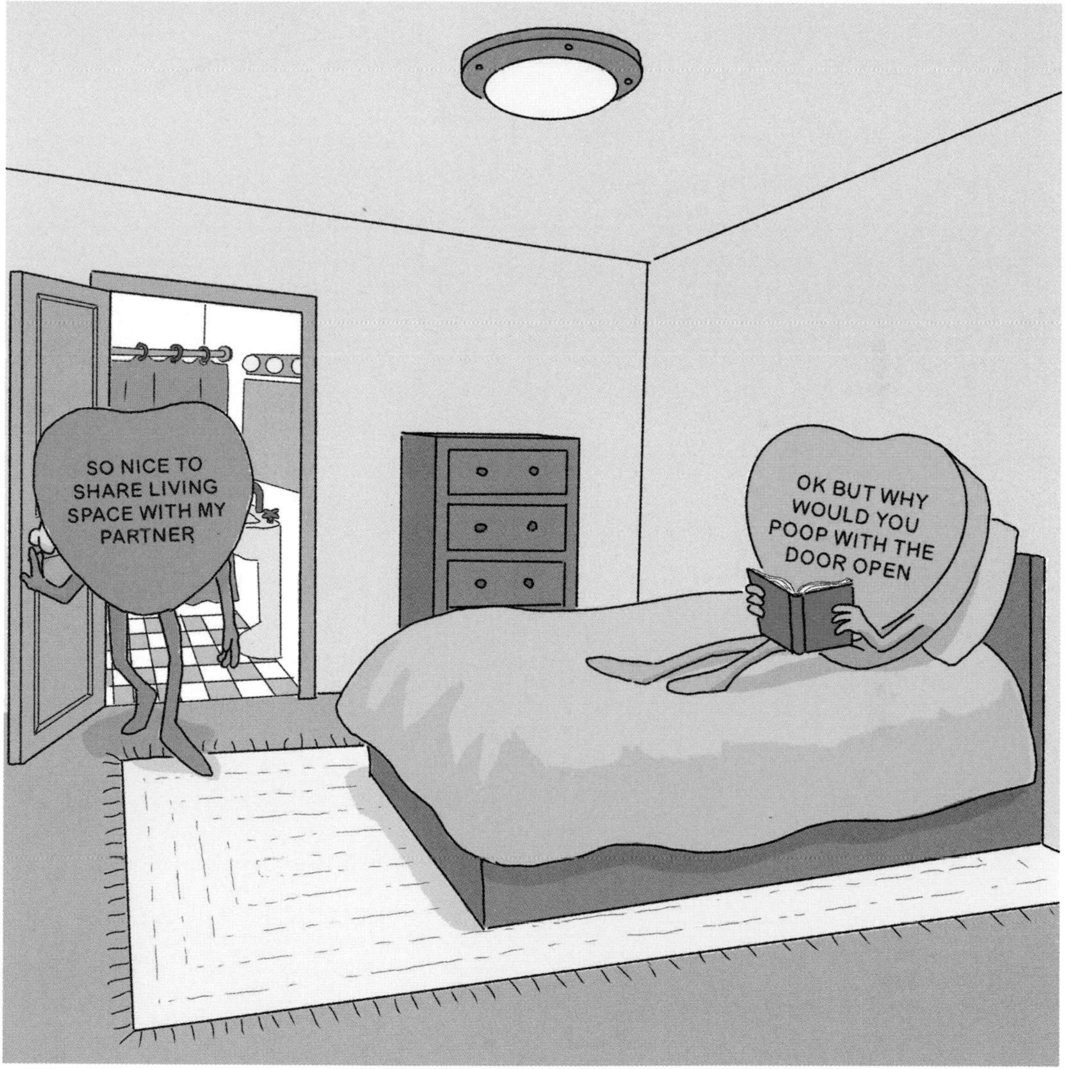
SO NICE TO SHARE LIVING SPACE WITH MY PARTNER
OK BUT WHY WOULD YOU POOP WITH THE DOOR OPEN

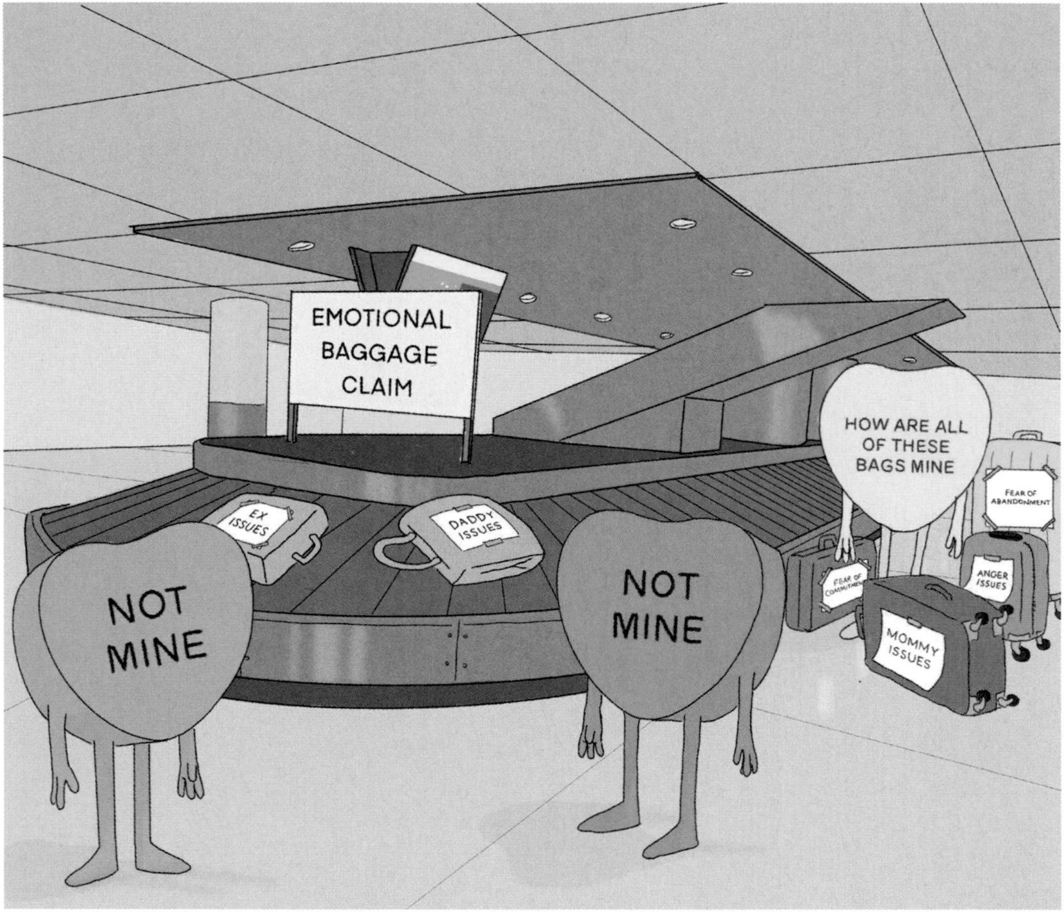
EMOTIONAL BAGGAGE CLAIM
EX ISSUES
DADDY ISSUES
NOT MINE
NOT MINE
HOW ARE ALL OF THESE BAGS MINE
FEAR OF ABANDONMENT
FEAR OF COMMITMEN
ANGER ISSUES
MOMMY ISSUES

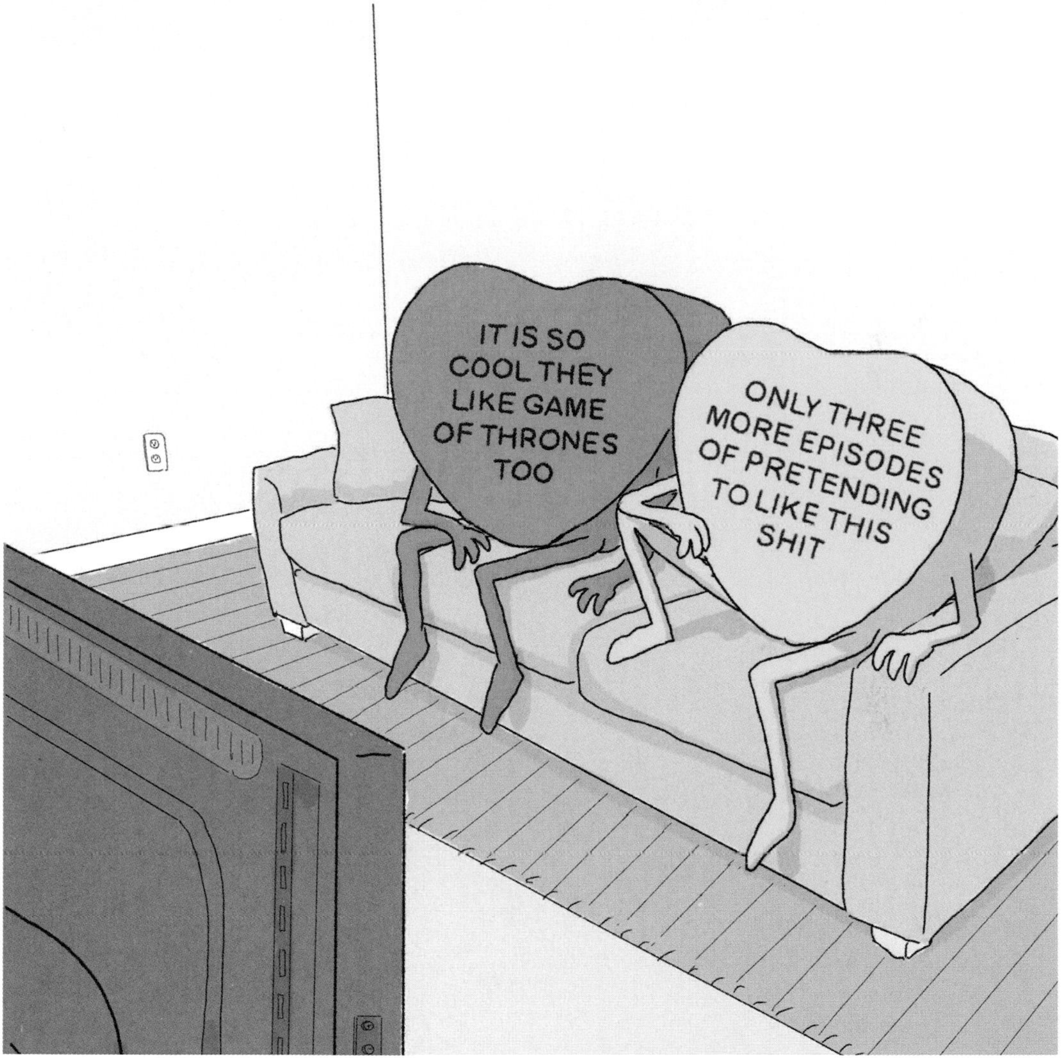
IT IS SO COOL THEY LIKE GAME OF THRONES TOO
ONLY THREE MORE EPISODES OF PRETENDING TO LIKE THIS SHIT

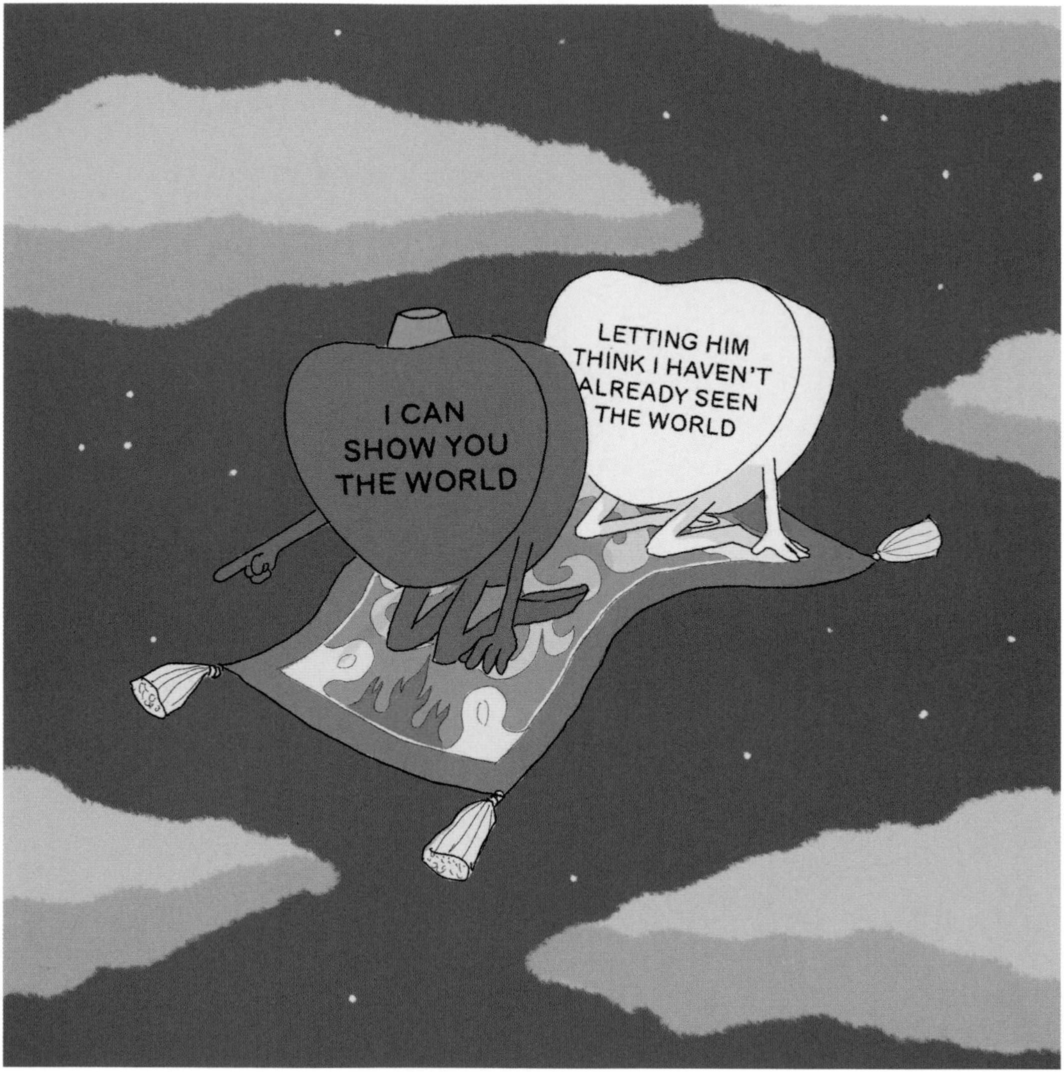
I CAN
SHOW YOU
THE WORLD
LETTING HIM
THINK I HAVEN'T
ALREADY SEEN
THE WORLD

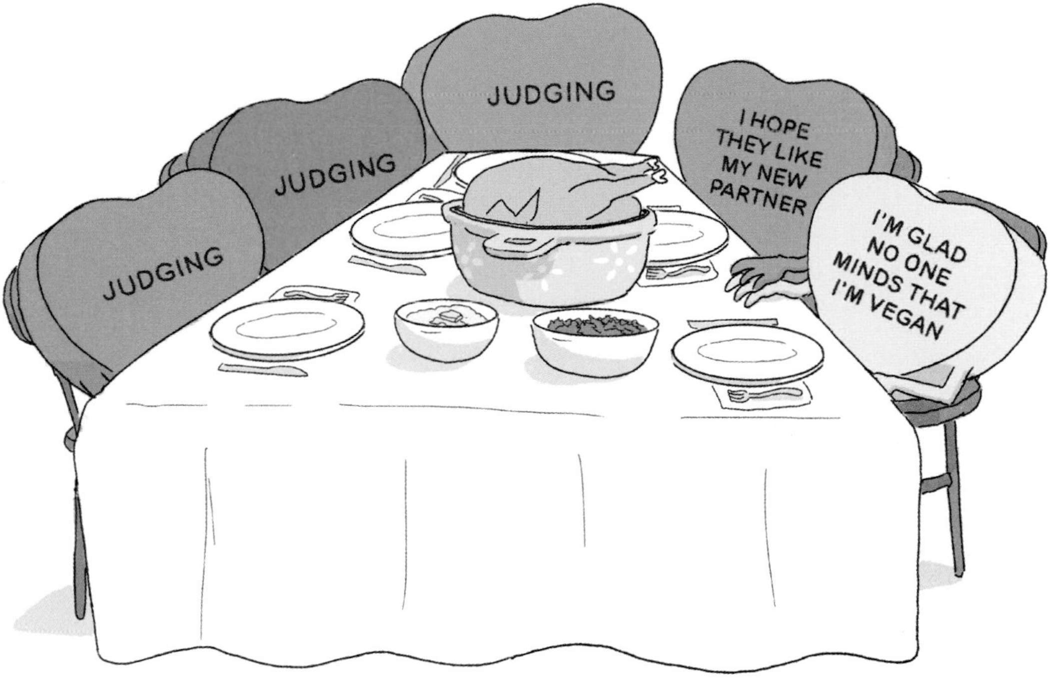
JUDGING
JUDGING
JUDGING
I HOPE THEY LIKE MY NEW PARTNER
I'M GLAD NO ONE MINDS THAT I'M VEGAN

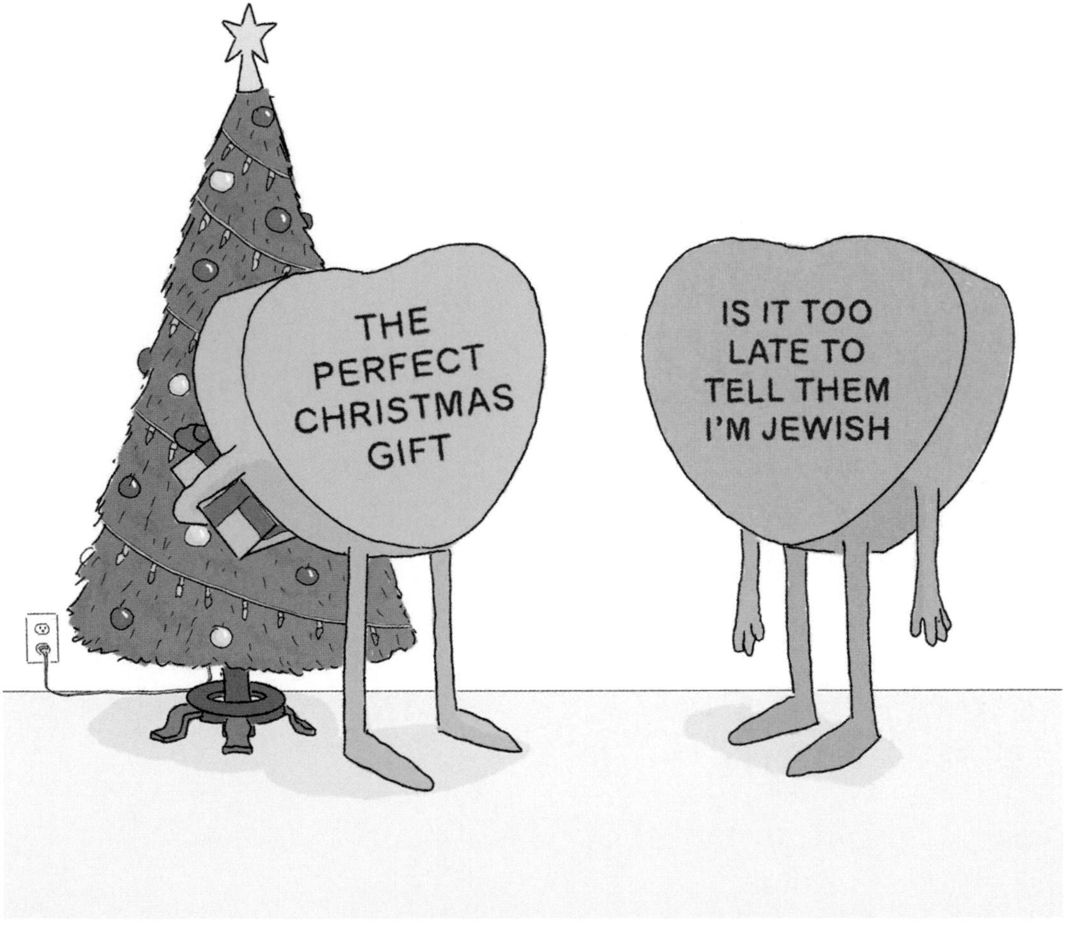
THE PERFECT CHRISTMAS GIFT
IS IT TOO LATE TO TELL THEM I'M JEWISH

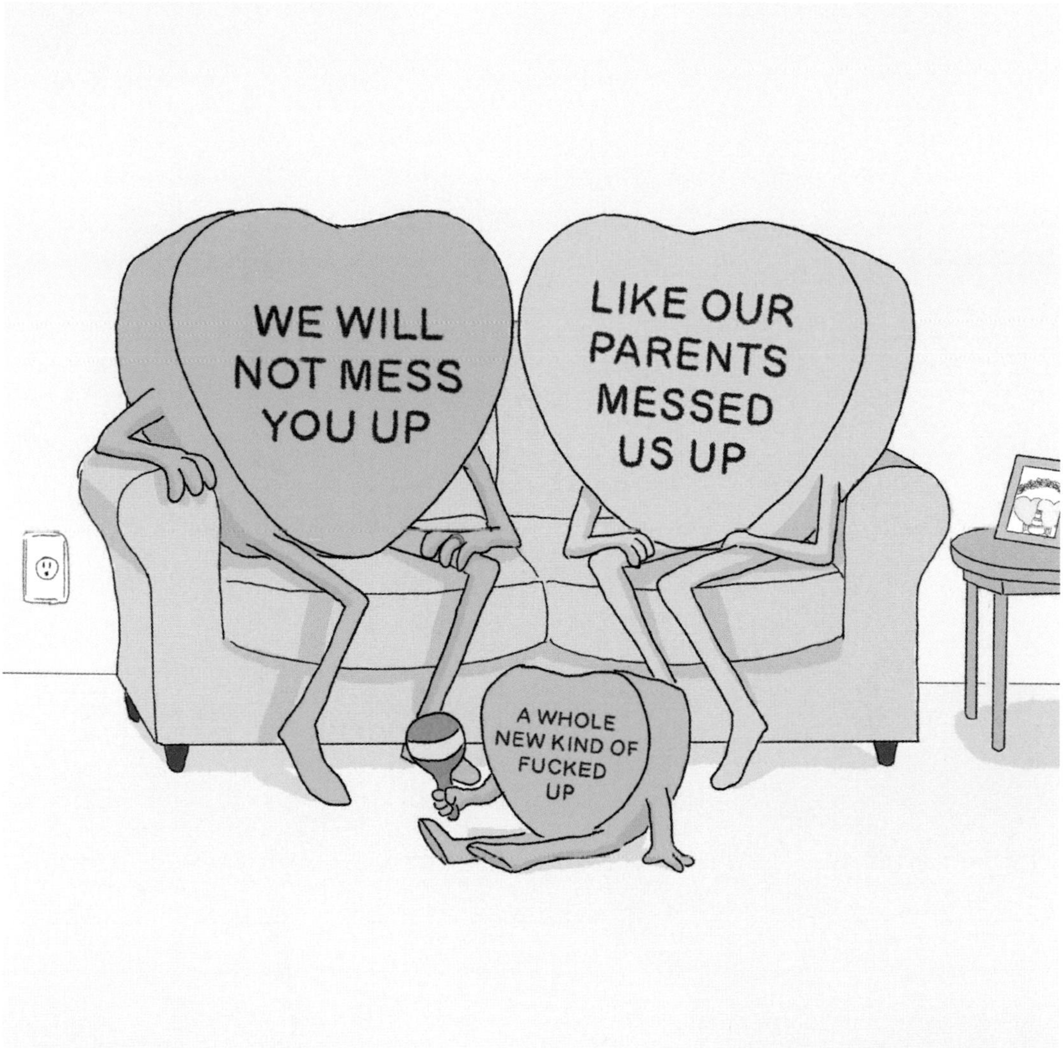
WE WILL NOT MESS YOU UP
LIKE OUR PARENTS MESSED US UP
A WHOLE NEW KIND OF FUCKED UP

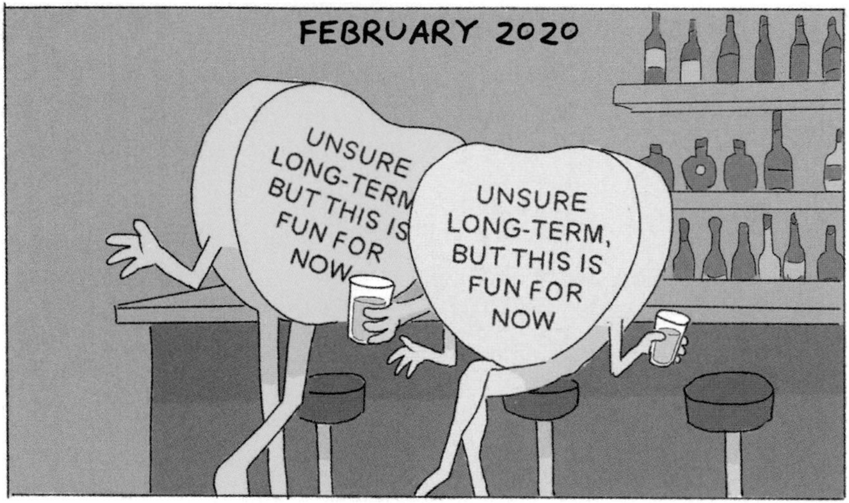
FEBRUARY 2020
UNSURE LONG-TERM BUT THIS IS FUN FOR NOW
UNSURE LONG-TERM, BUT THIS IS FUN FOR NOW

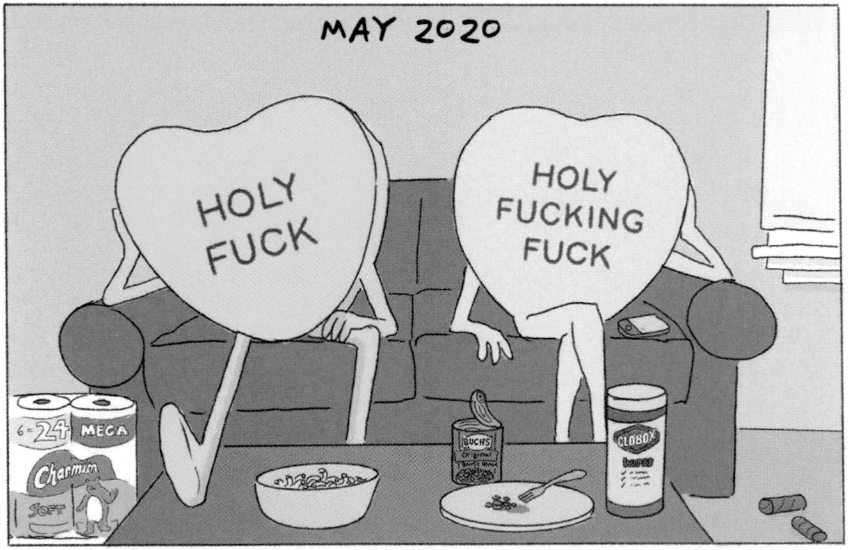
MAY 2020
HOLY FUCK
HOLY FUCKING FUCK
6=24 MEGA
SOFT
BUCHS
CLOBOX

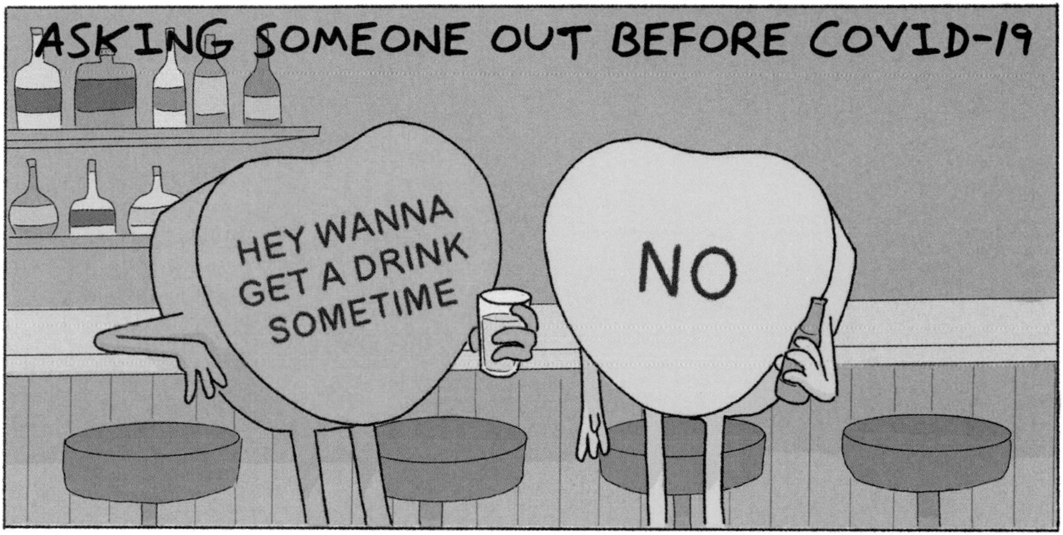
ASKING SOMEONE OUT BEFORE COVID-19
HEY WANNA GET A DRINK SOMETIME
NO

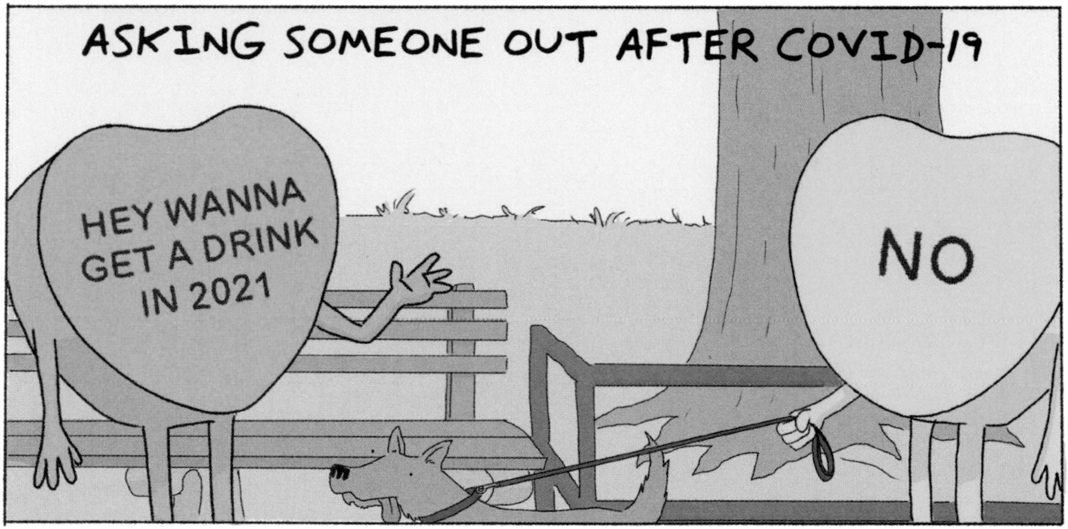
ASKING SOMEONE OUT AFTER COVID-19
HEY WANNA GET A DRINK IN 2021
NO

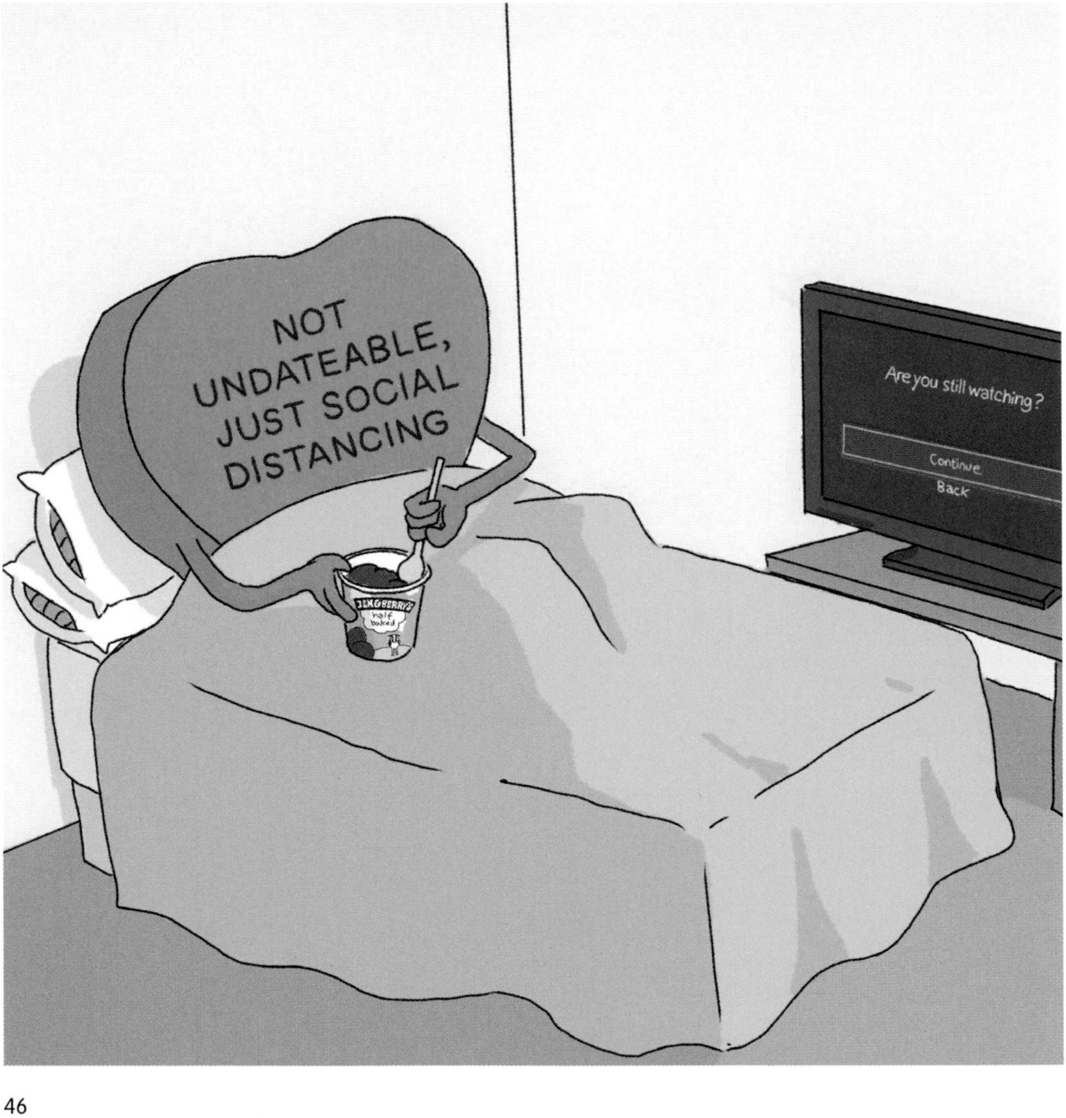
NOT UNDATEABLE, JUST SOCIAL DISTANCING
Are you still watching?
Continue
Back

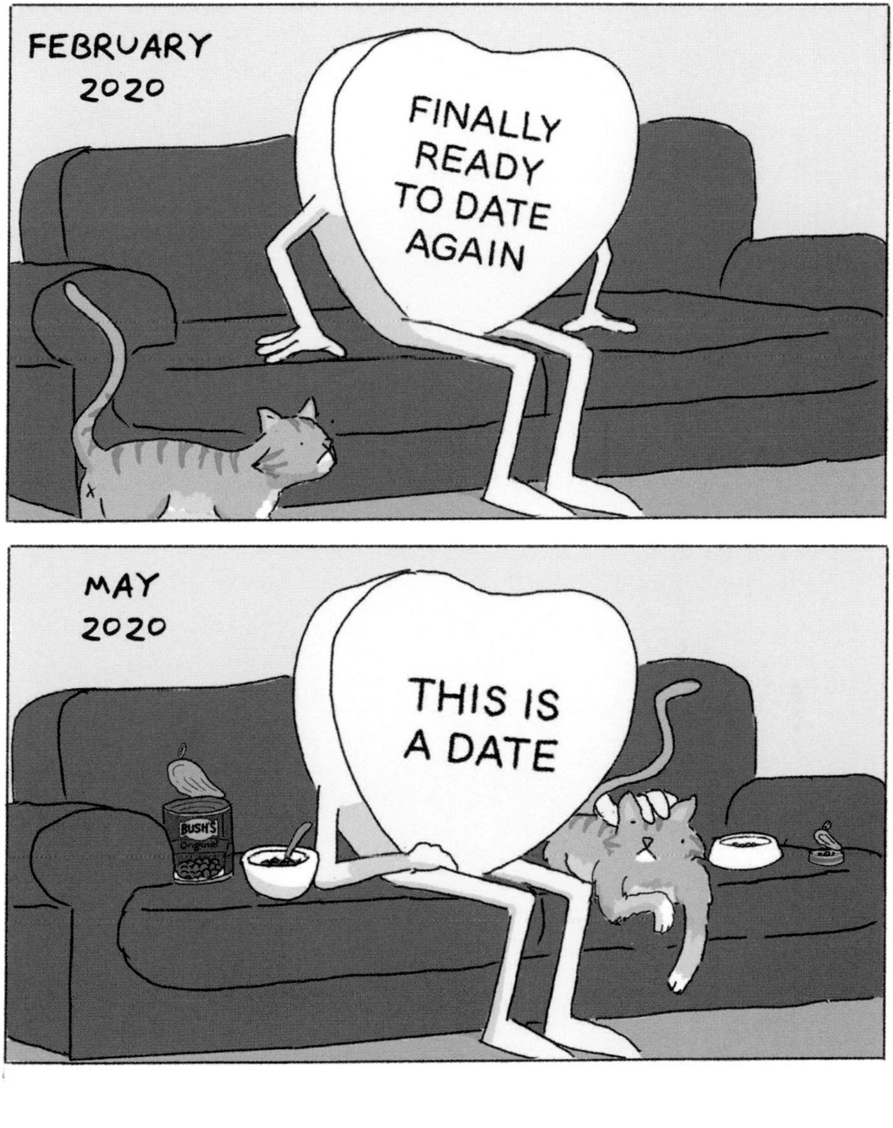
FEBRUARY 2020
FINALLY READY TO DATE AGAIN
MAY 2020
THIS IS A DATE
BUSH'S

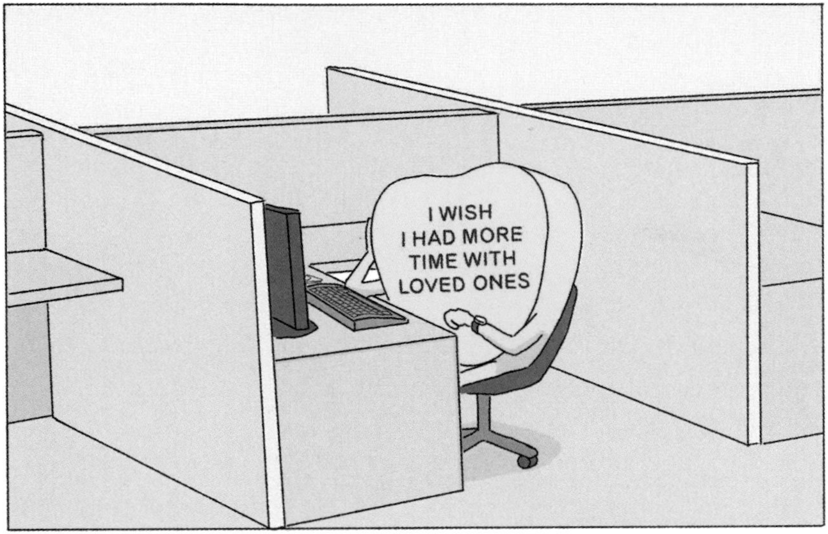
I WISH
I HAD MORE
TIME WITH
LOVED ONES

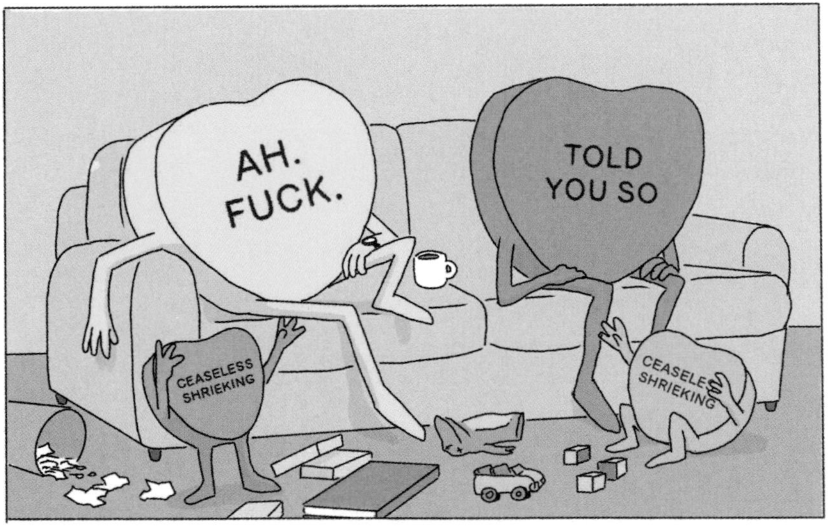
AH.
FUCK.
TOLD
YOU SO
CEASELESS
SHRIEKING
CEASELESS
SHRIEKING

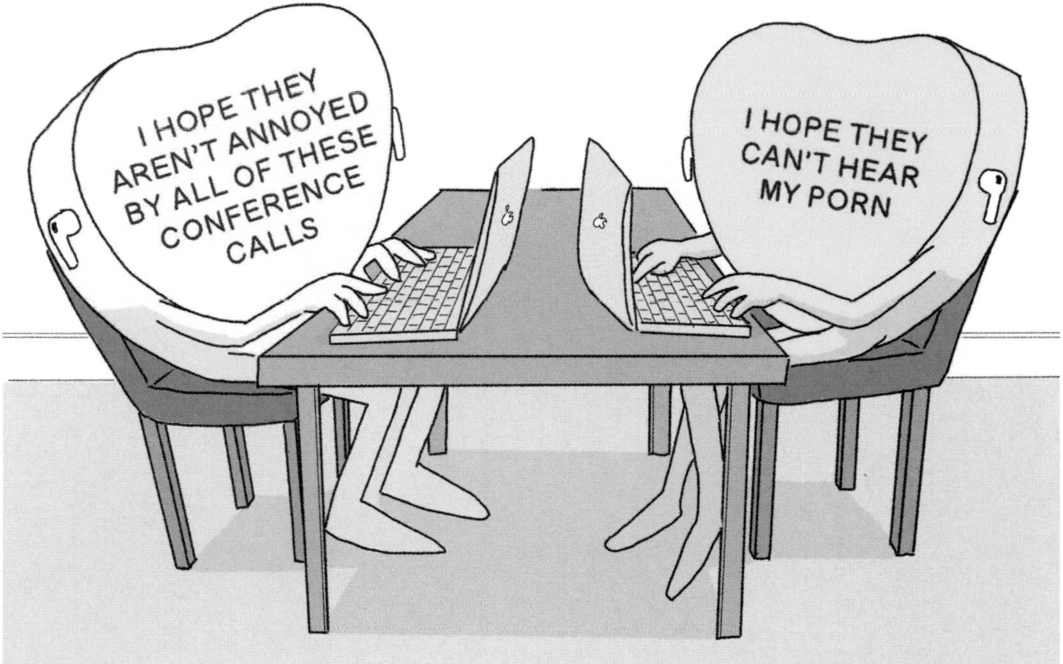
I HOPE THEY AREN'T ANNOYED BY ALL OF THESE CONFERENCE CALLS
I HOPE THEY CAN'T HEAR MY PORN

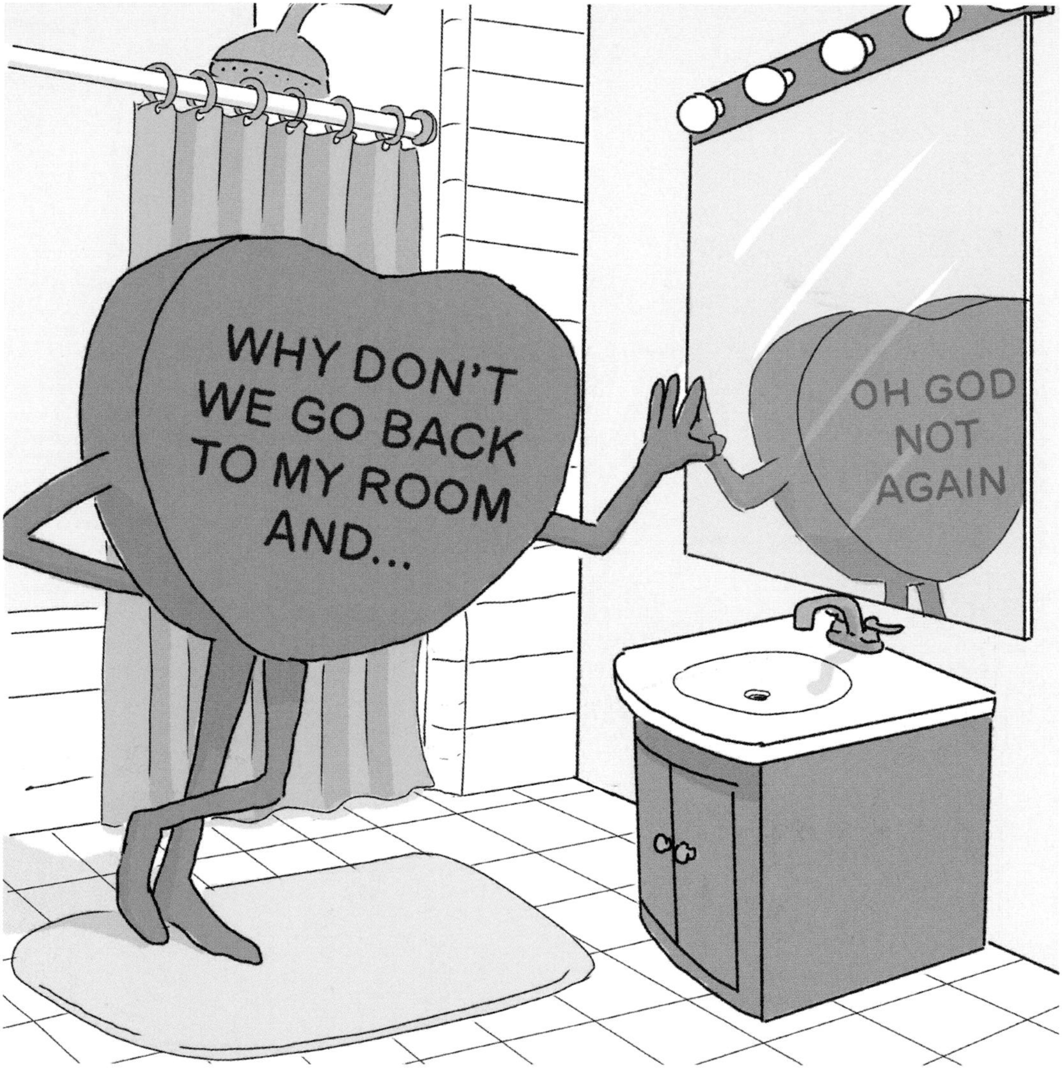
WHY DON'T WE GO BACK TO MY ROOM AND...
OH GOD NOT AGAIN

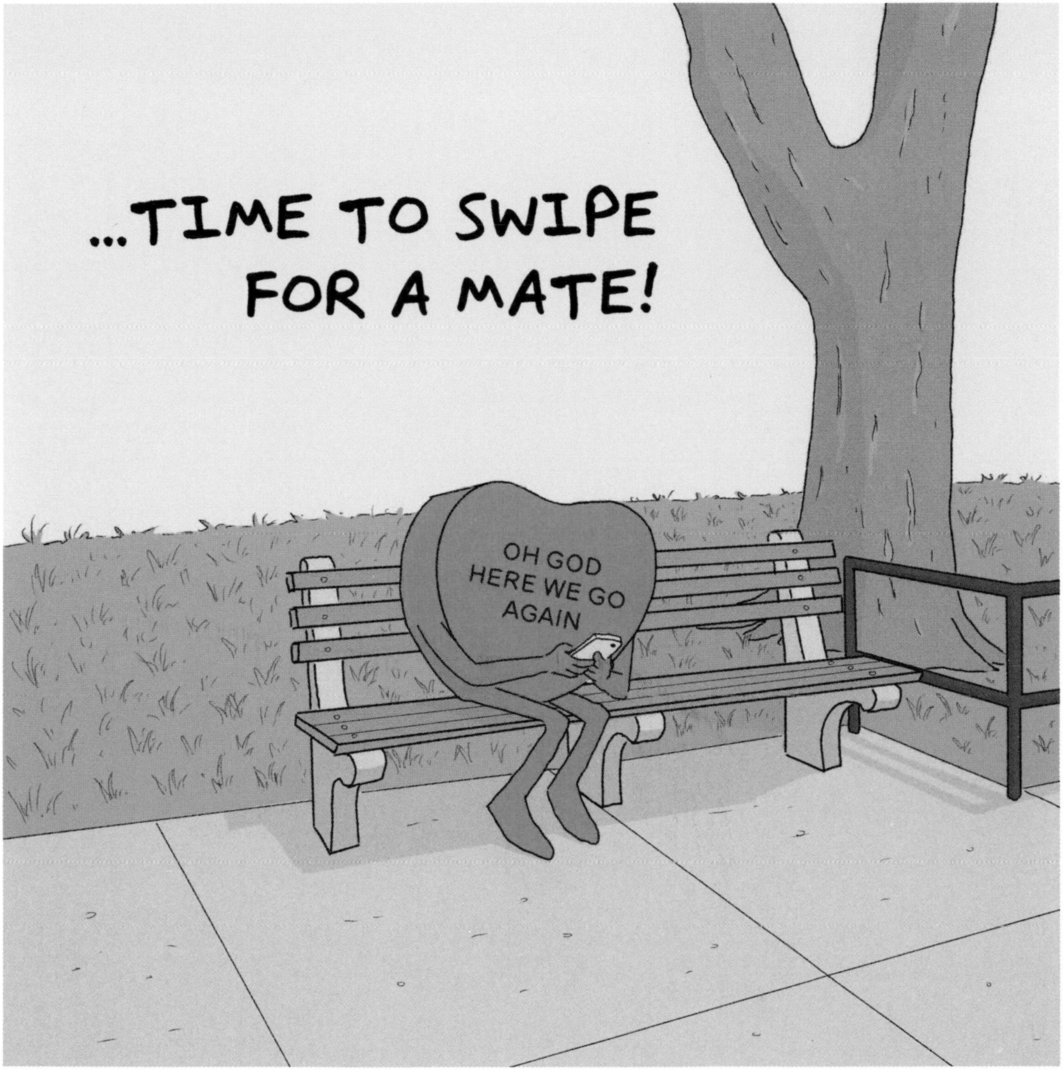
...TIME TO SWIPE
FOR A MATE!
OH GOD
HERE WE GO
AGAIN

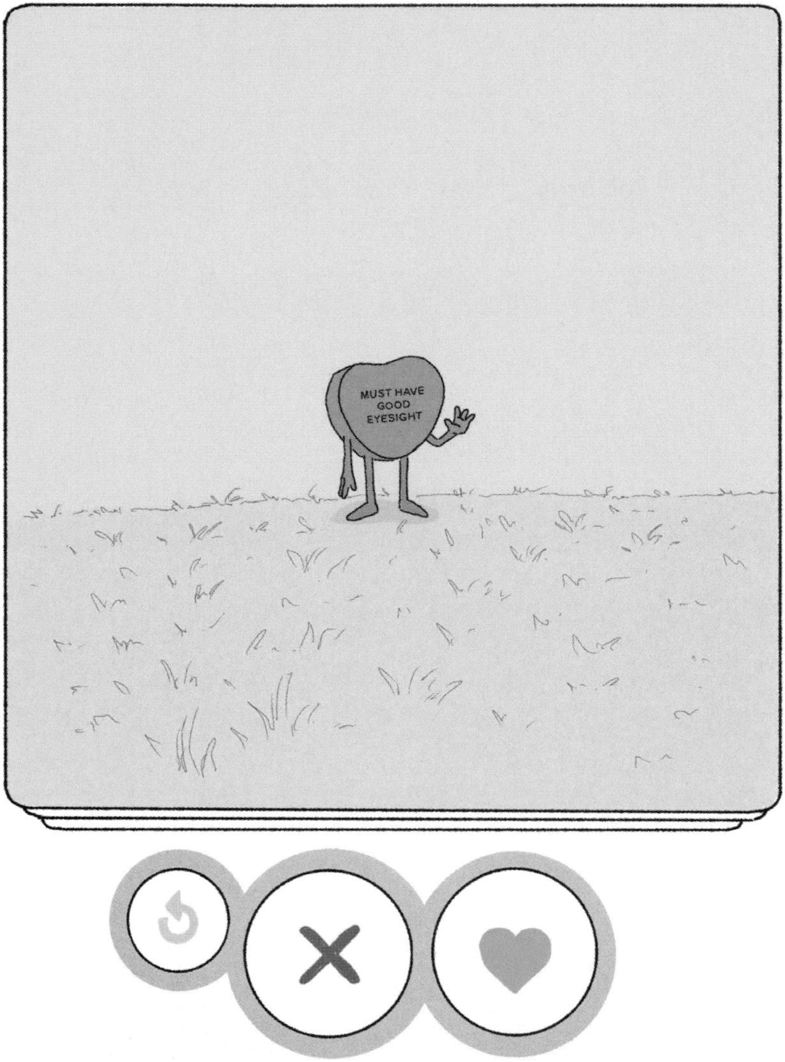
MUST HAVE
GOOD
EYESIGHT

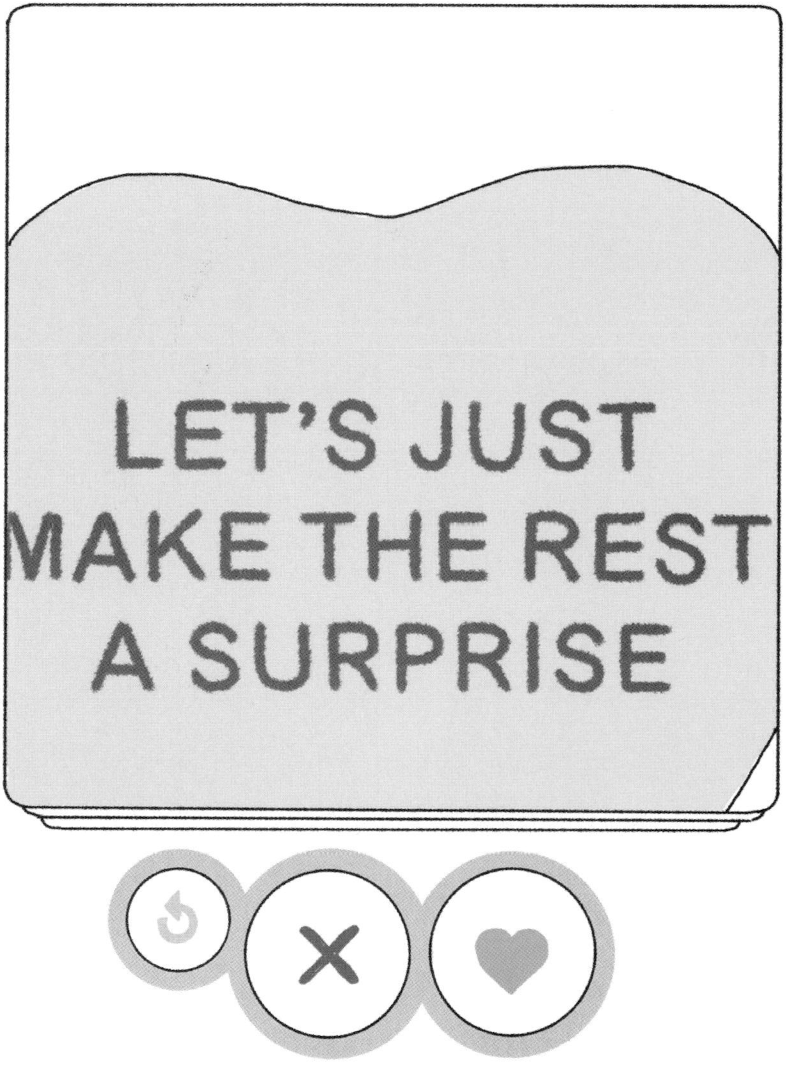
LET'S JUST
MAKE THE REST
A SURPRISE

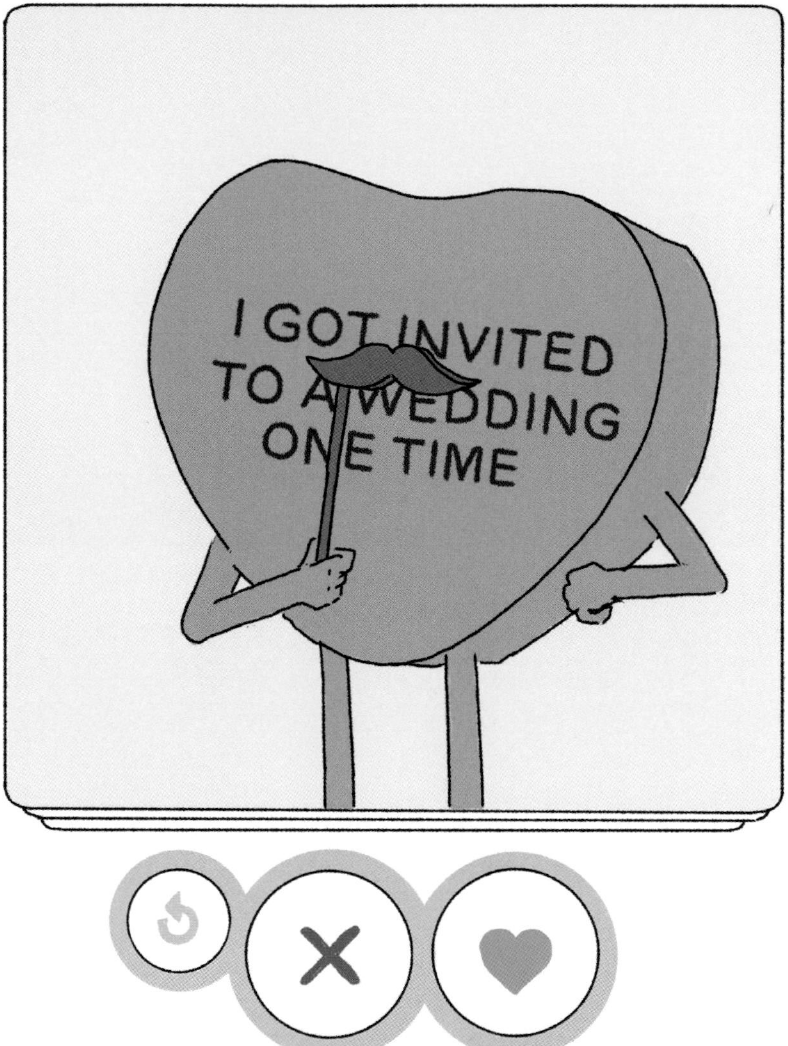
I GOT INVITED
TO A WEDDING
ONE TIME

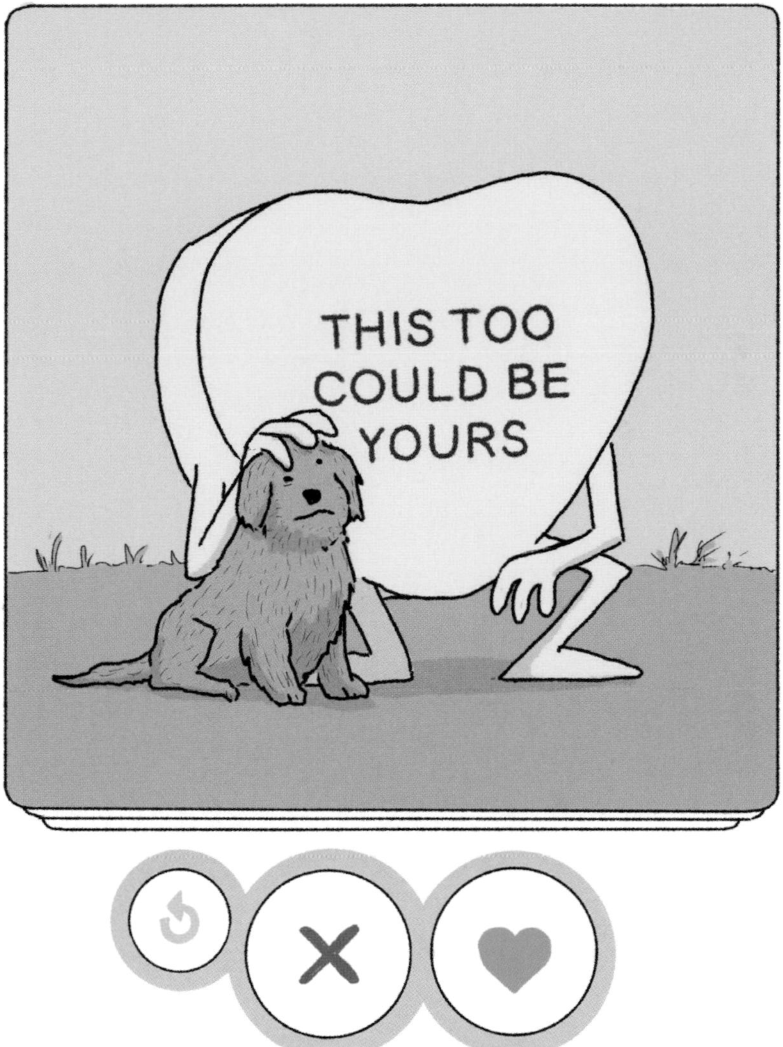
THIS TOO
COULD BE
YOURS

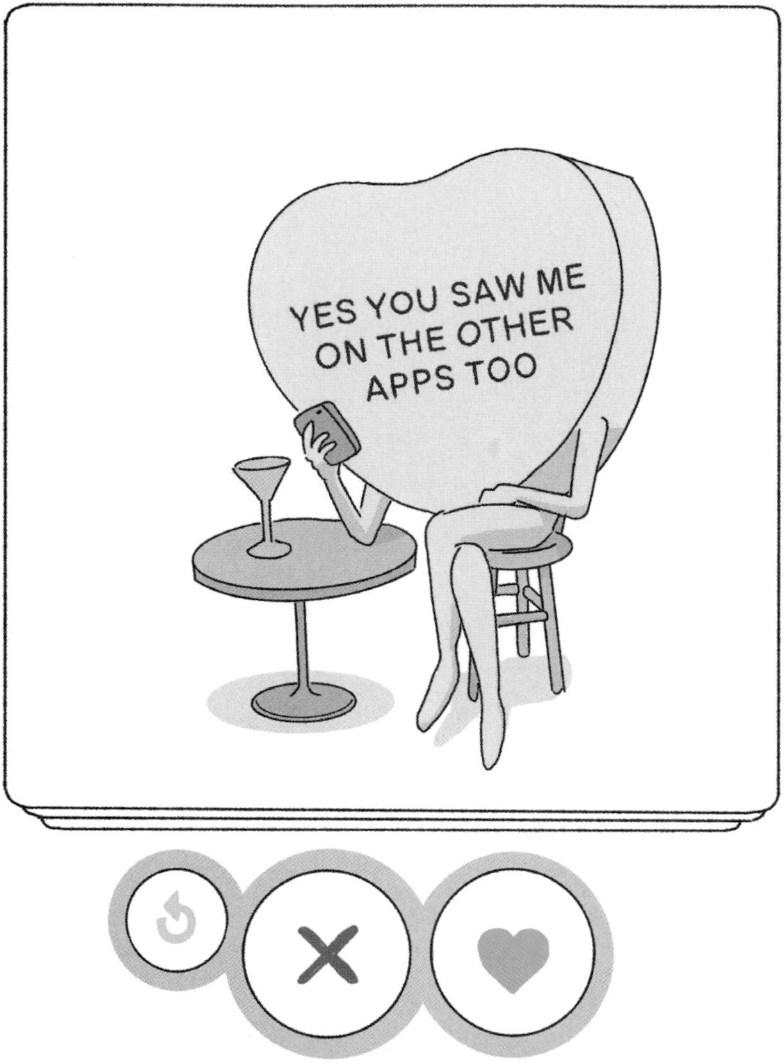
YES YOU SAW ME
ON THE OTHER
APPS TOO

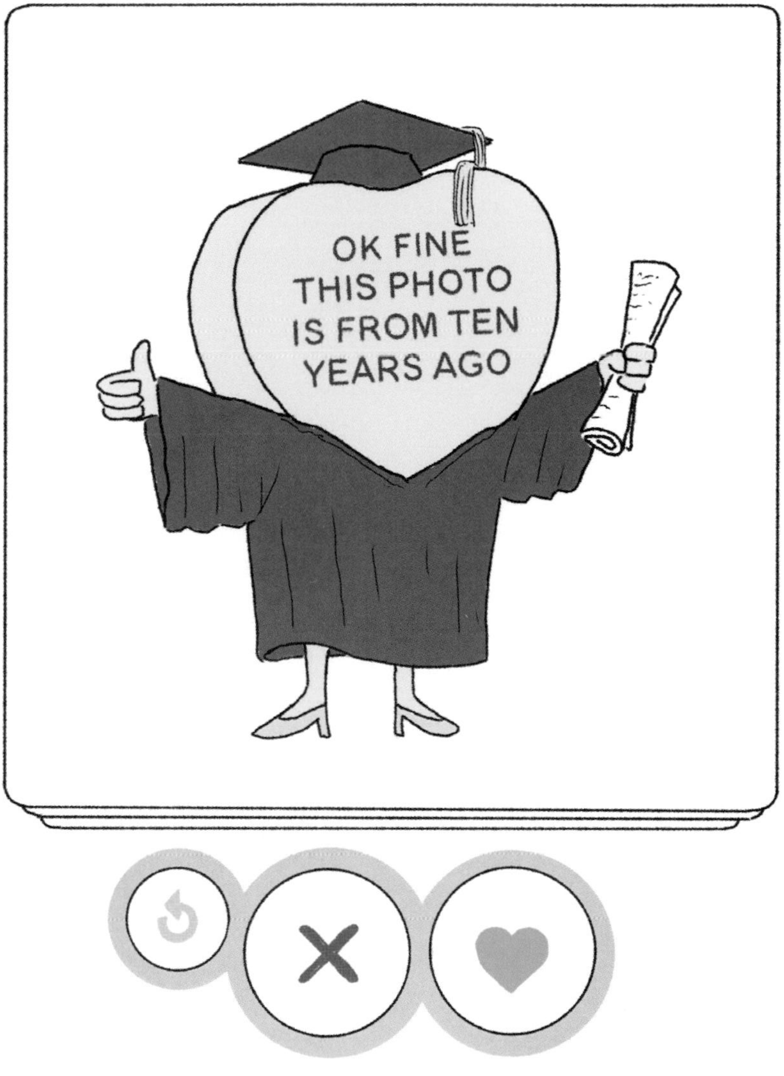
OK FINE
THIS PHOTO
IS FROM TEN
YEARS AGO

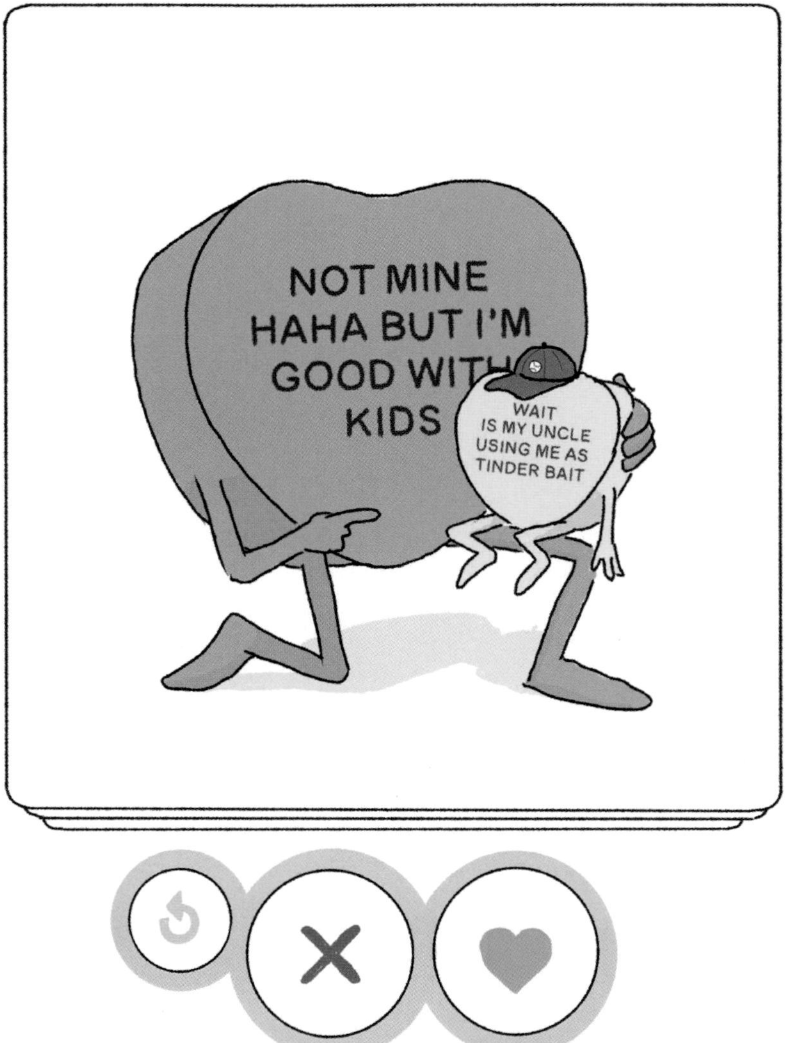
NOT MINE
HAHA BUT I'M
GOOD WITH
KIDS
WAIT
IS MY UNCLE
USING ME AS
TINDER BAIT

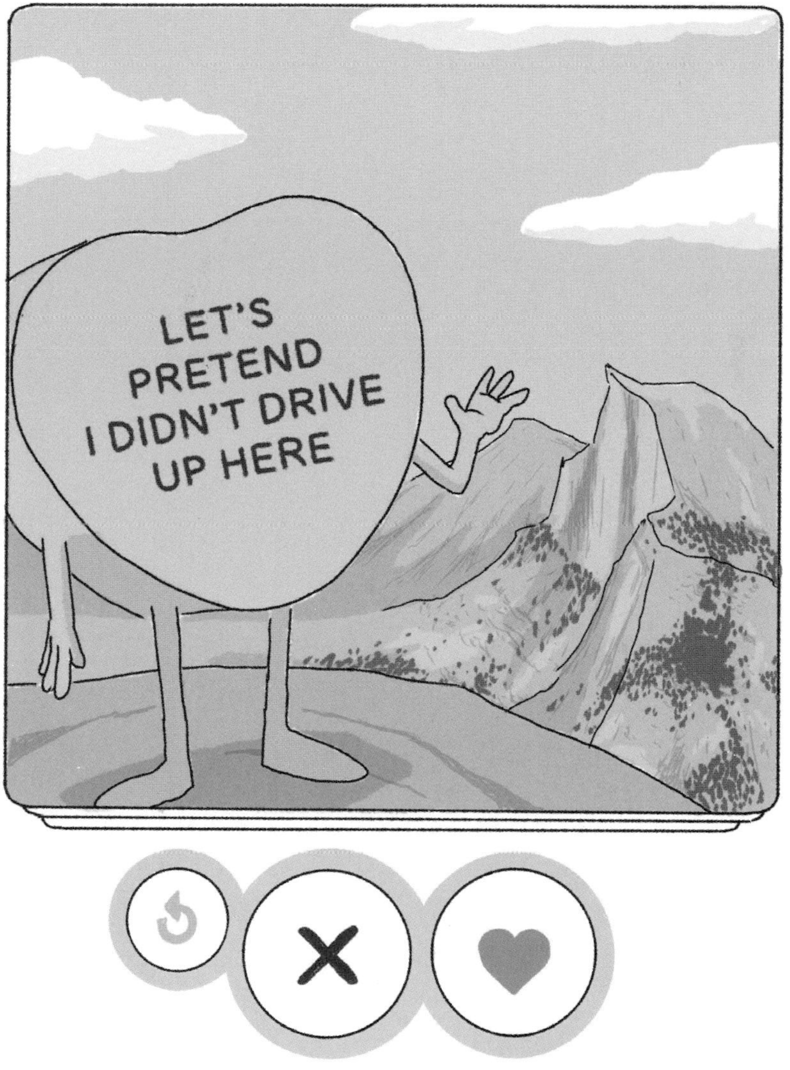
LET'S PRETEND I DIDN'T DRIVE UP HERE

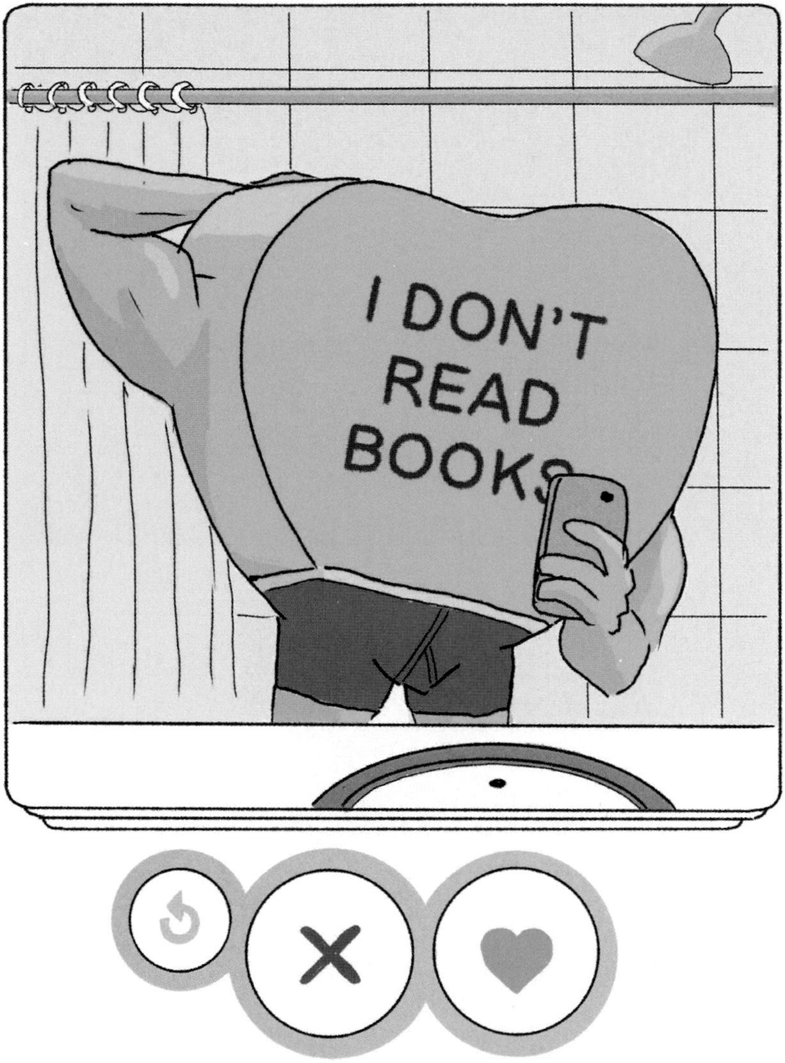
I DON'T
READ
BOOKS

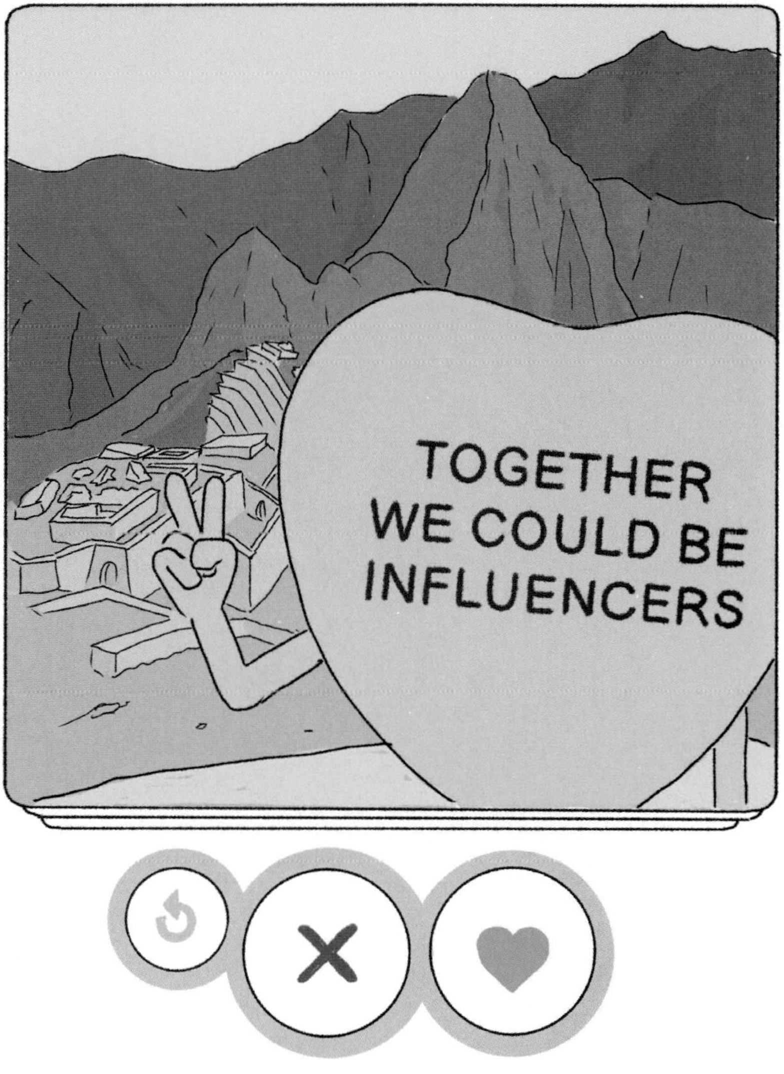
TOGETHER
WE COULD BE
INFLUENCERS

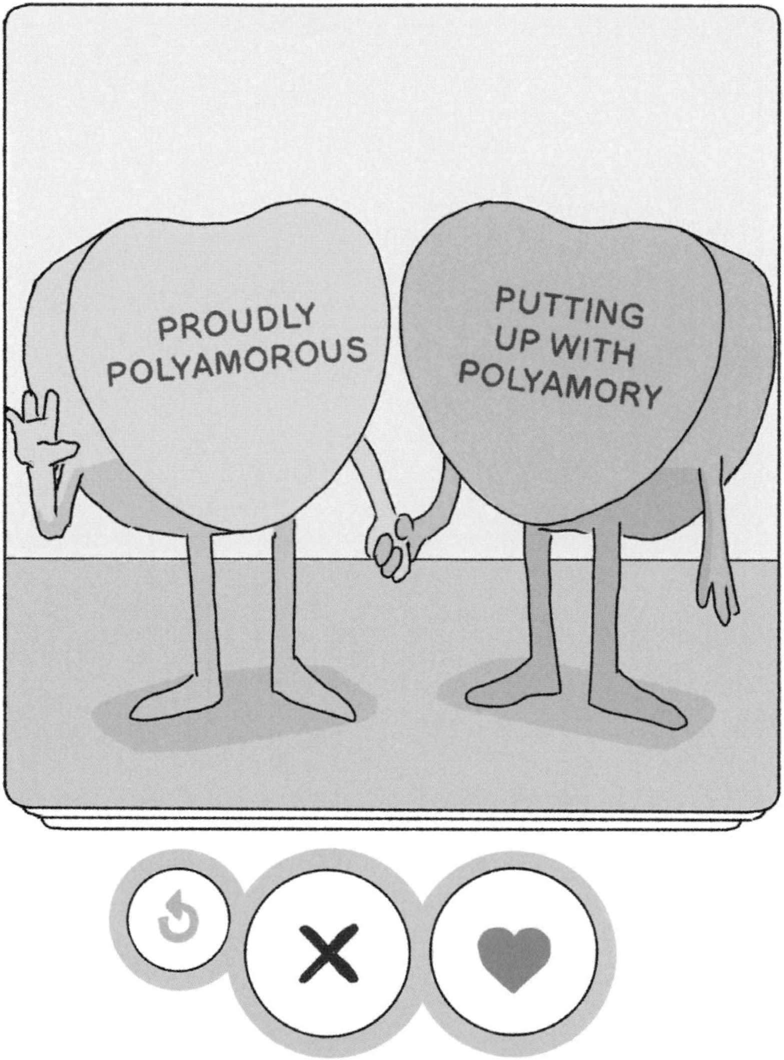
PROUDLY POLYAMOROUS
PUTTING UP WITH POLYAMORY

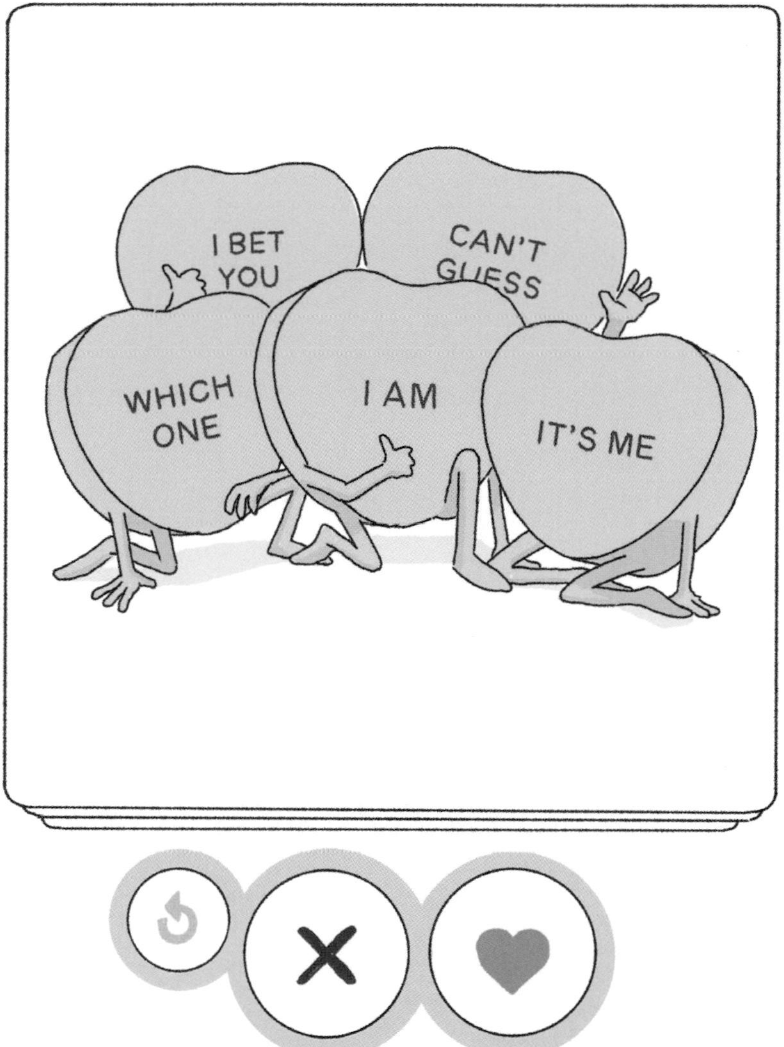
I BET YOU
CAN'T GUESS
WHICH ONE
I AM
IT'S ME

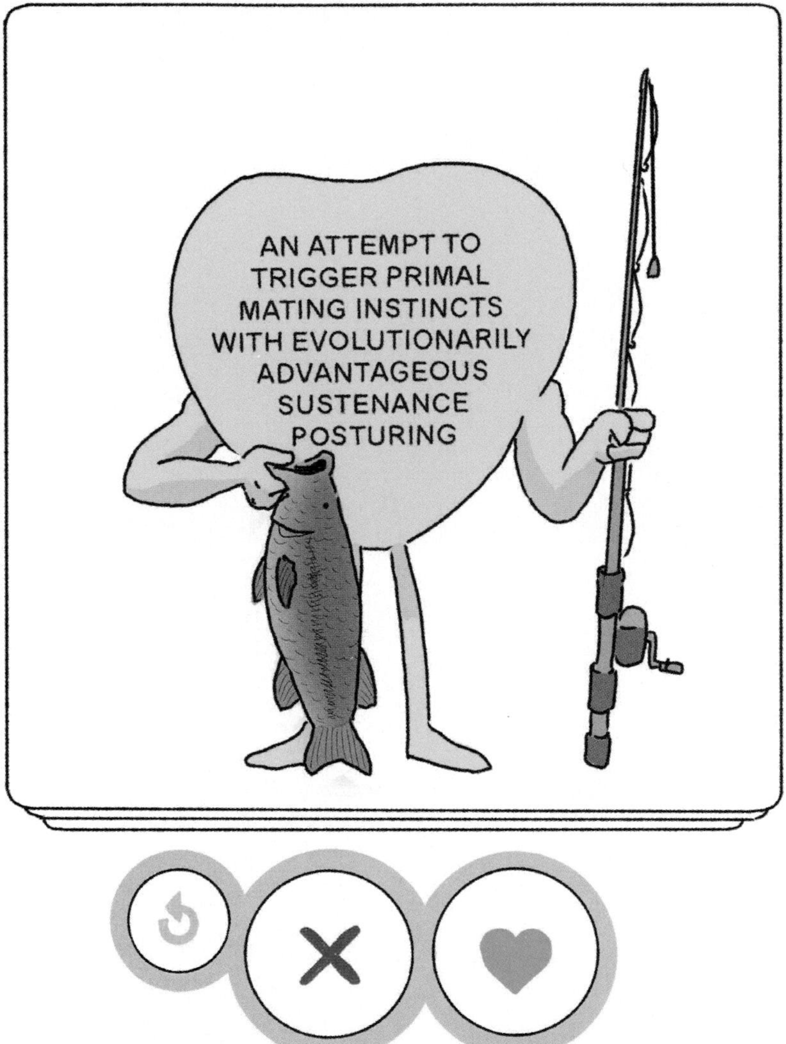
AN ATTEMPT TO TRIGGER PRIMAL MATING INSTINCTS WITH EVOLUTIONARILY ADVANTAGEOUS SUSTENANCE POSTURING

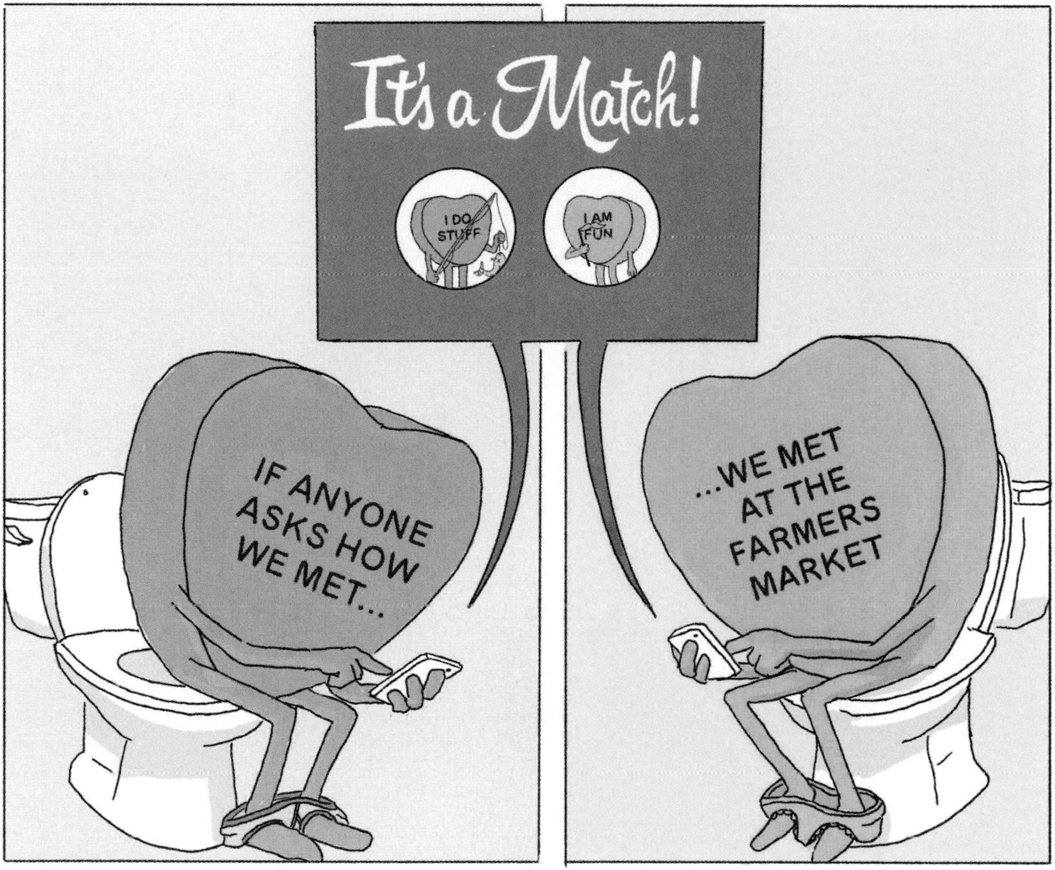
It's a Match!
I DO STUFF
I AM FUN
IF ANYONE ASKS HOW WE MET...
...WE MET AT THE FARMERS MARKET

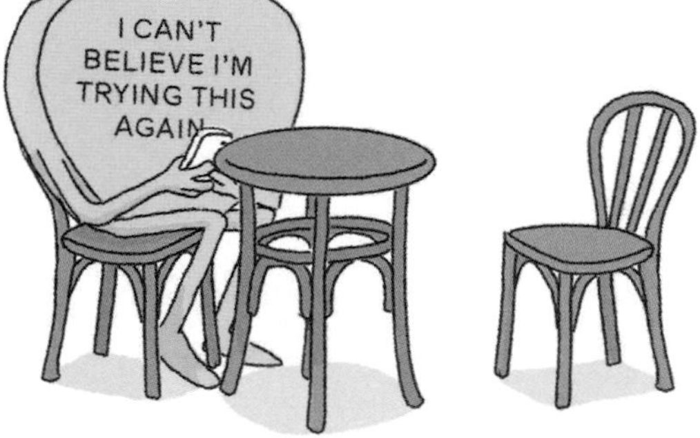
I CAN'T BELIEVE I'M TRYING THIS AGAIN

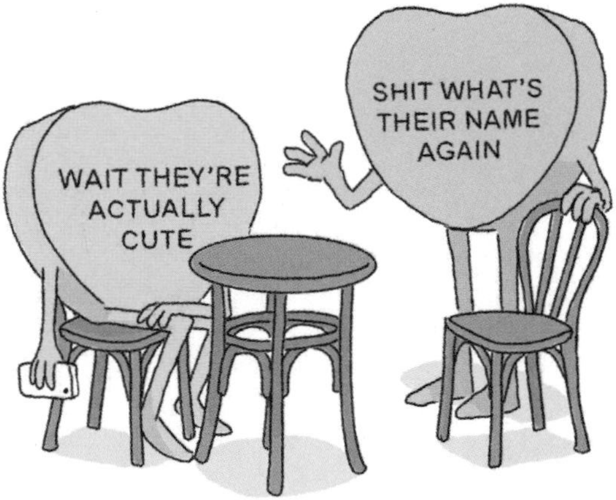
WAIT THEY'RE ACTUALLY CUTE
SHIT WHAT'S THEIR NAME AGAIN

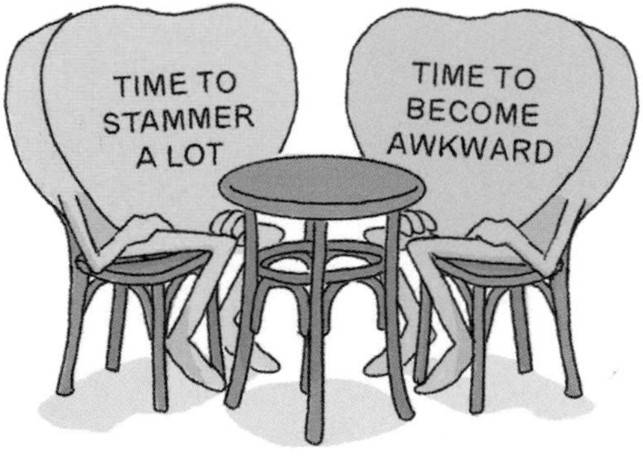
TIME TO STAMMER A LOT
TIME TO BECOME AWKWARD

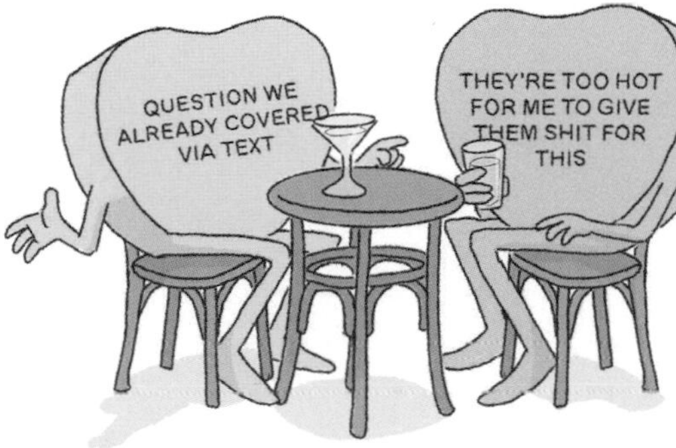
QUESTION WE ALREADY COVERED VIA TEXT
THEY'RE TOO HOT FOR ME TO GIVE THEM SHIT FOR THIS

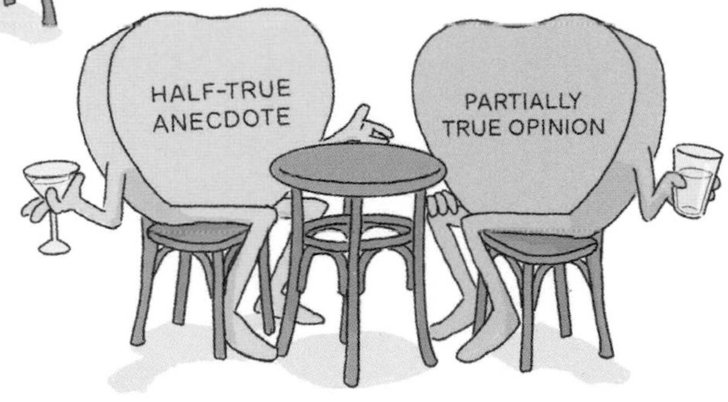
HALF-TRUE ANECDOTE
PARTIALLY TRUE OPINION

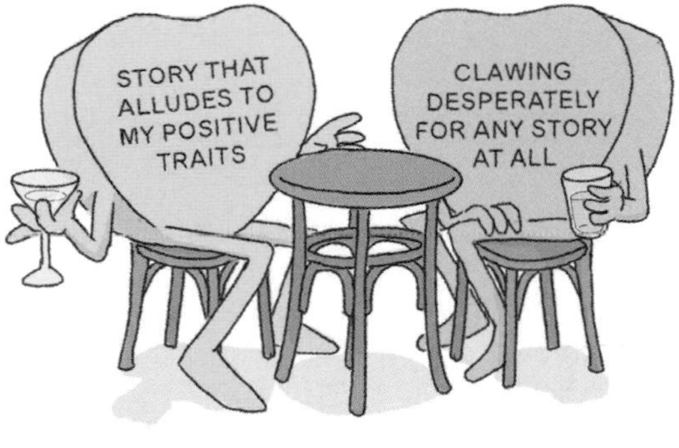
STORY THAT ALLUDES TO MY POSITIVE TRAITS
CLAWING DESPERATELY FOR ANY STORY AT ALL

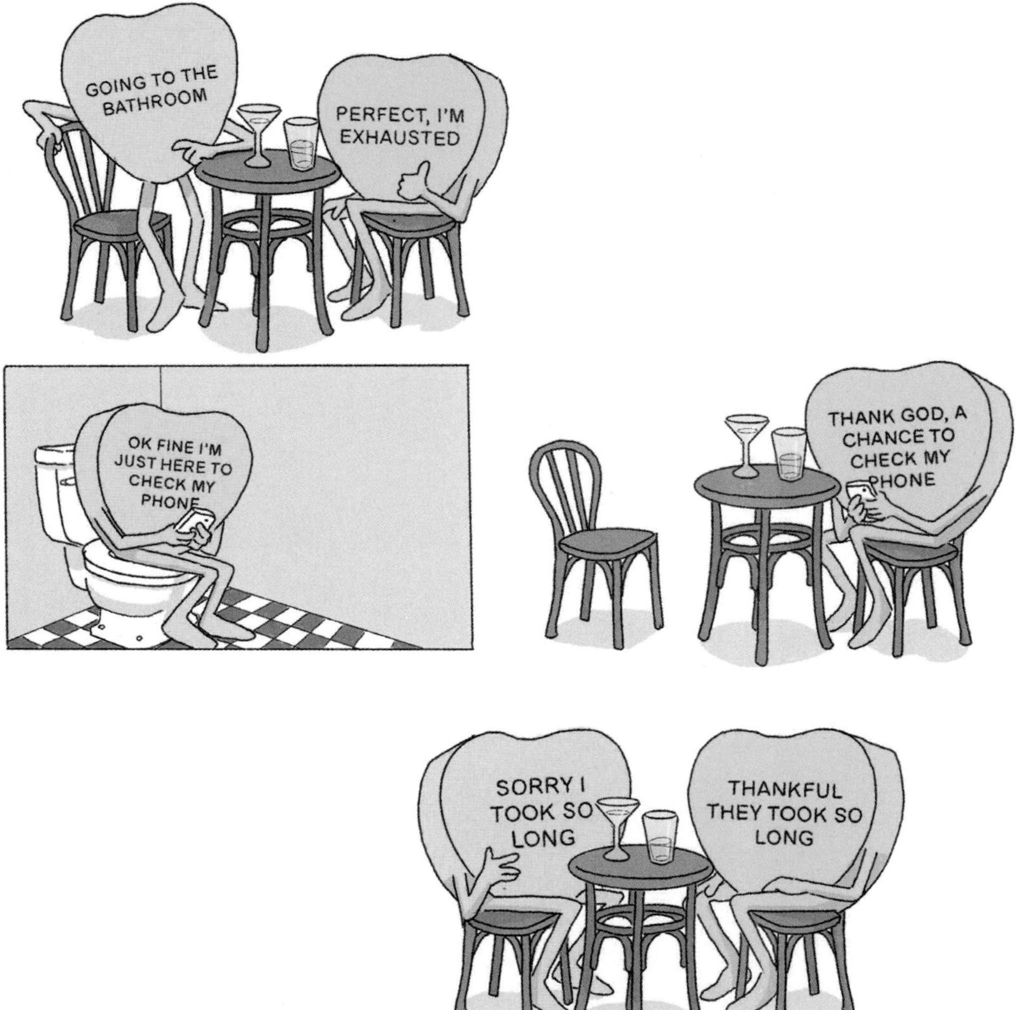
GOING TO THE BATHROOM
PERFECT, I'M EXHAUSTED
OK FINE I'M JUST HERE TO CHECK MY PHONE
THANK GOD, A CHANCE TO CHECK MY PHONE
SORRY I TOOK SO LONG
THANKFUL THEY TOOK SO LONG

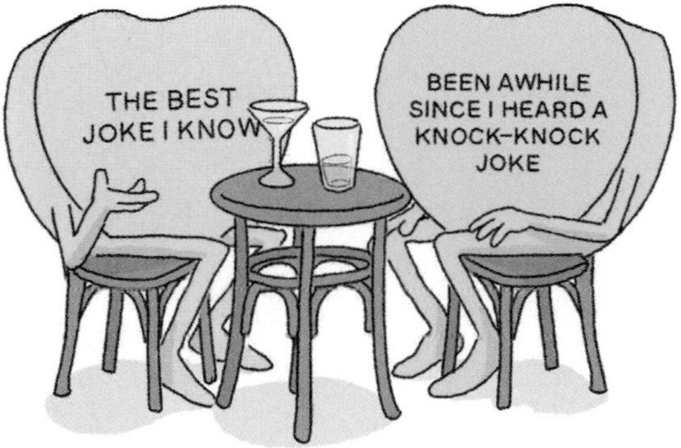
THE BEST JOKE I KNOW
BEEN AWHILE SINCE I HEARD A KNOCK-KNOCK JOKE

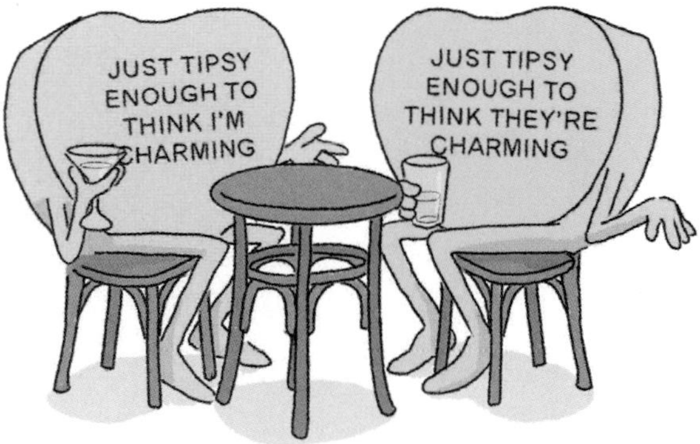
JUST TIPSY ENOUGH TO THINK I'M CHARMING
JUST TIPSY ENOUGH TO THINK THEY'RE CHARMING

THIS IS SO FUN I COULD TALK ALL NIGHT
OMG I COULD TOO

FOR THE LOVE OF GOD PLEASE LEAVE

...
...

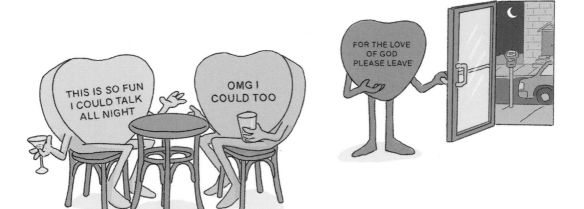

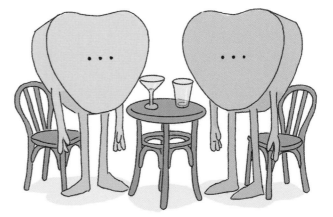

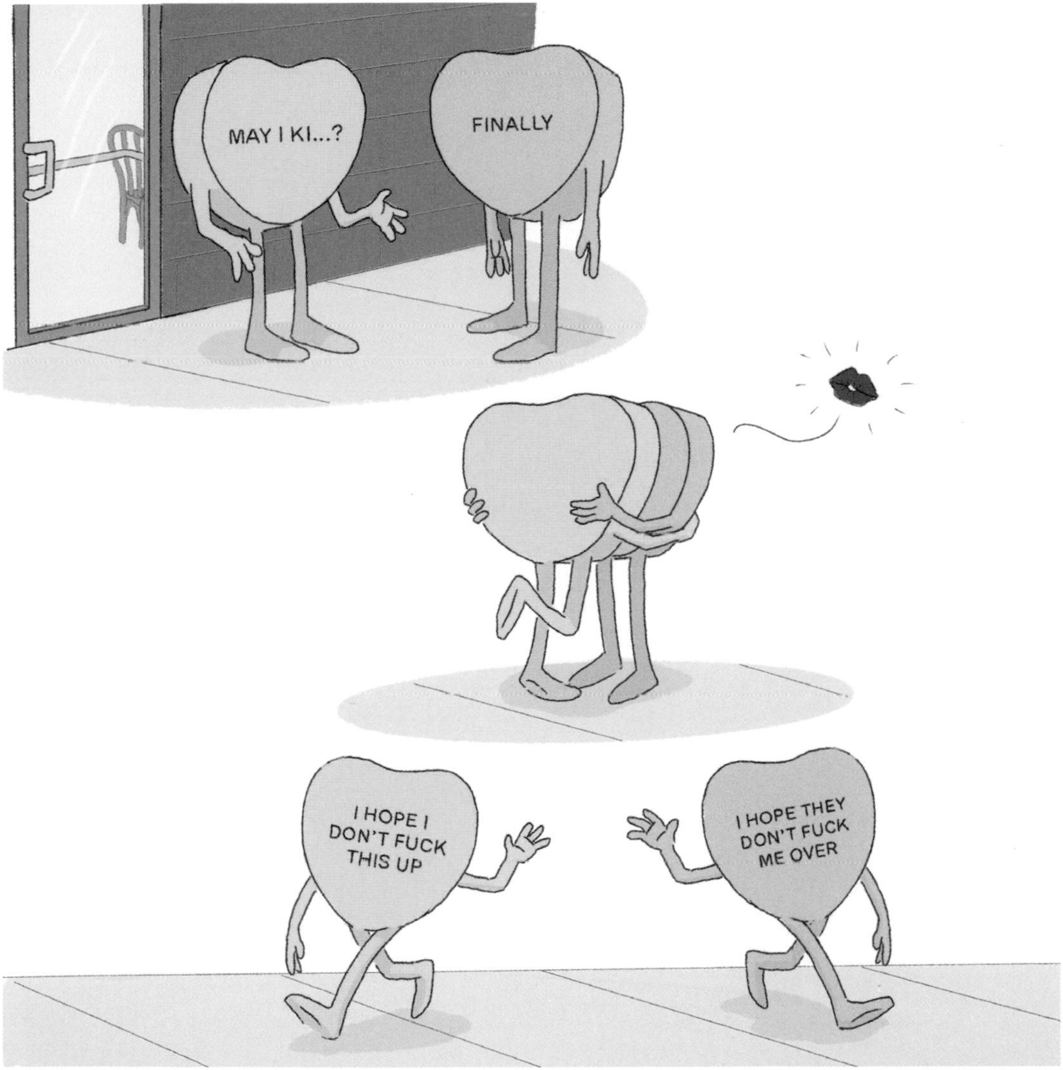
MAY I KI...?
FINALLY
I HOPE I DON'T FUCK THIS UP
I HOPE THEY DON'T FUCK ME OVER

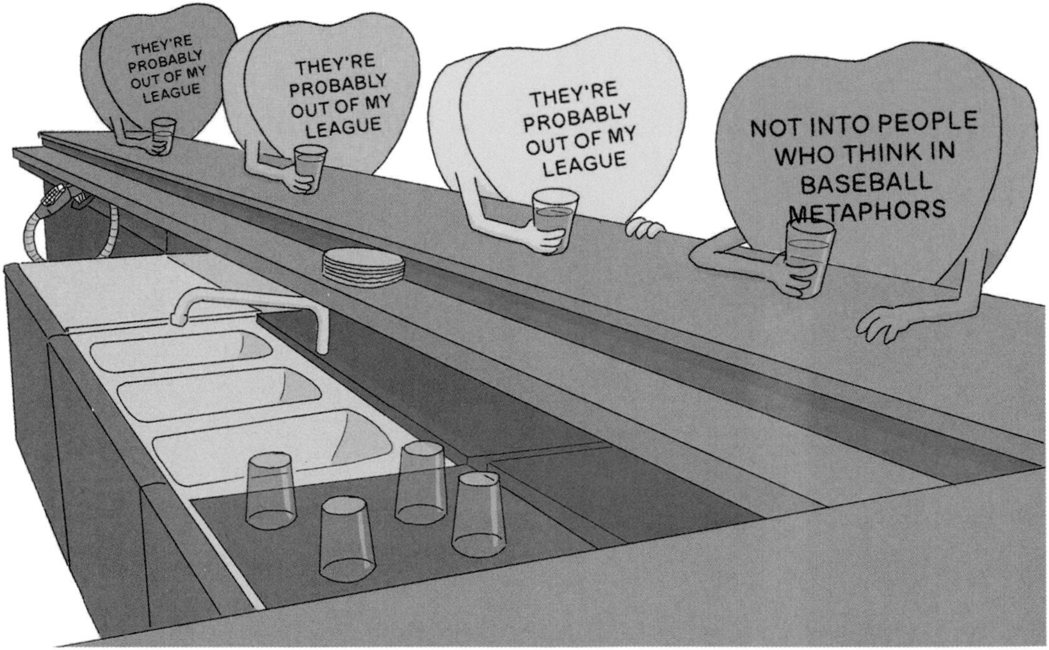
THEY'RE PROBABLY OUT OF MY LEAGUE
THEY'RE PROBABLY OUT OF MY LEAGUE
THEY'RE PROBABLY OUT OF MY LEAGUE
NOT INTO PEOPLE WHO THINK IN BASEBALL METAPHORS

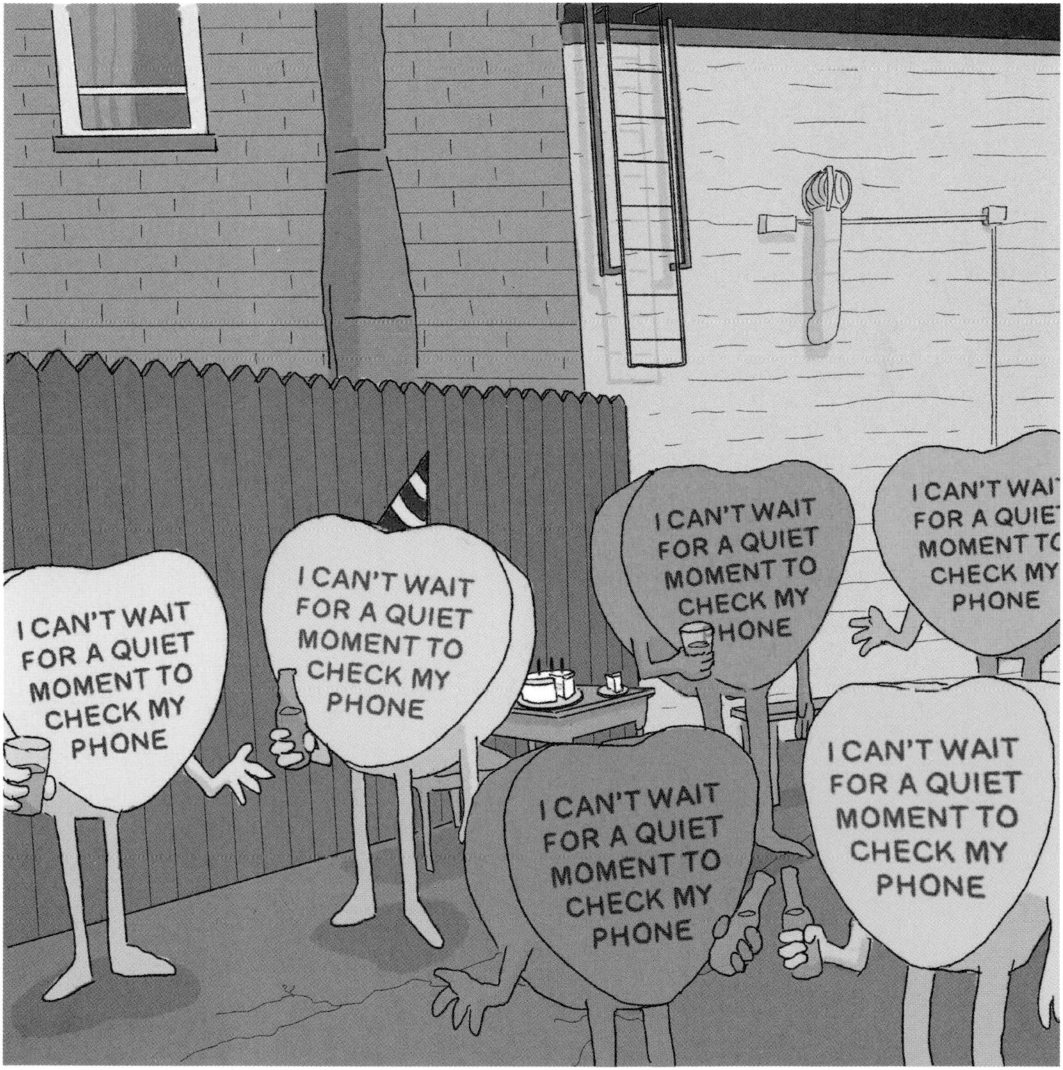
I CAN'T WAIT FOR A QUIET MOMENT TO CHECK MY PHONE
I CAN'T WAIT FOR A QUIET MOMENT TO CHECK MY PHONE
I CAN'T WAIT FOR A QUIET MOMENT TO CHECK MY HONE
I CAN'T WAI FOR A QUIE MOMENT TO CHECK MY PHONE
I CAN'T WAIT FOR A QUIET MOMENT TO CHECK MY PHONE
I CAN'T WAIT FOR A QUIET MOMENT TO CHECK MY PHONE

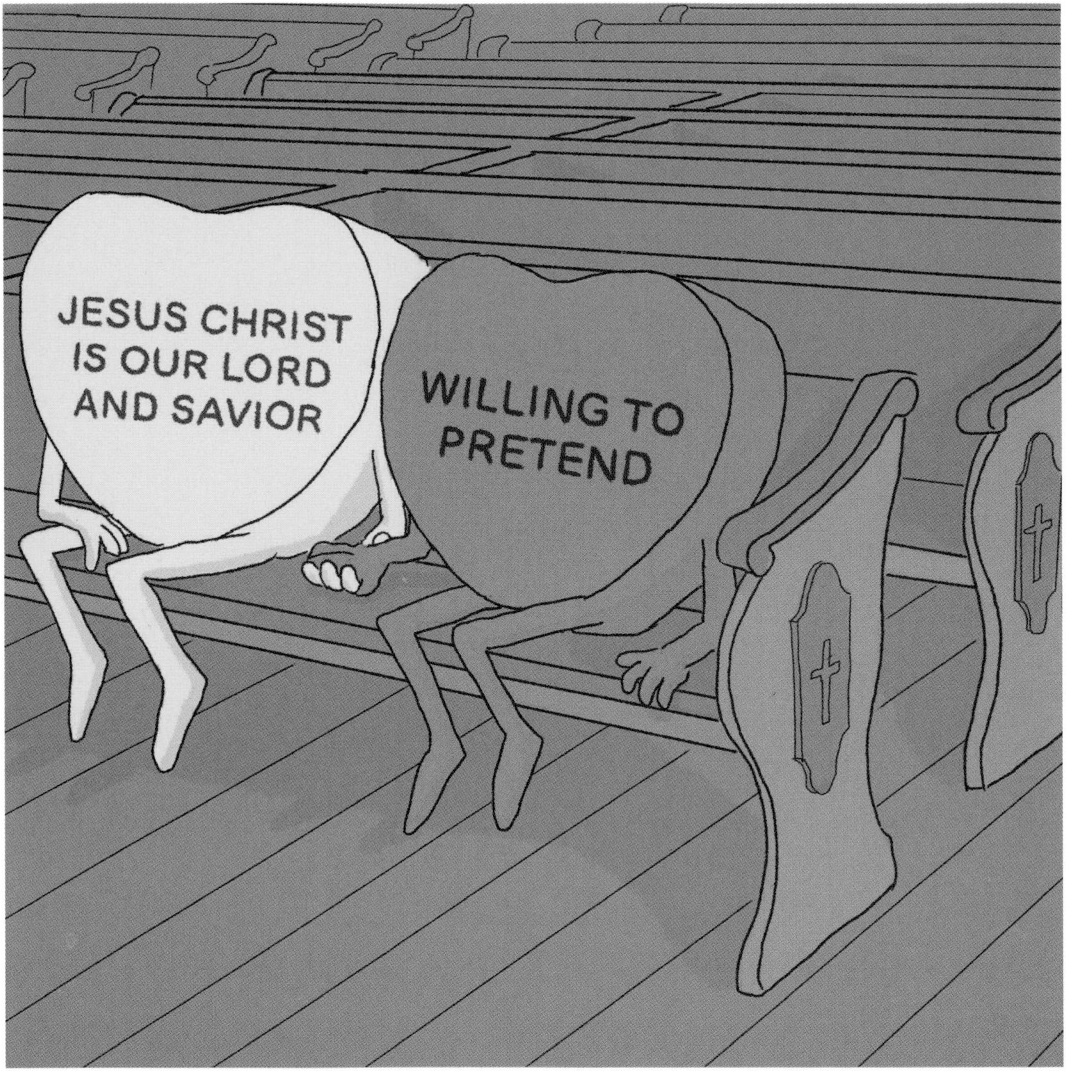
JESUS CHRIST
IS OUR LORD
AND SAVIOR
WILLING TO
PRETEND

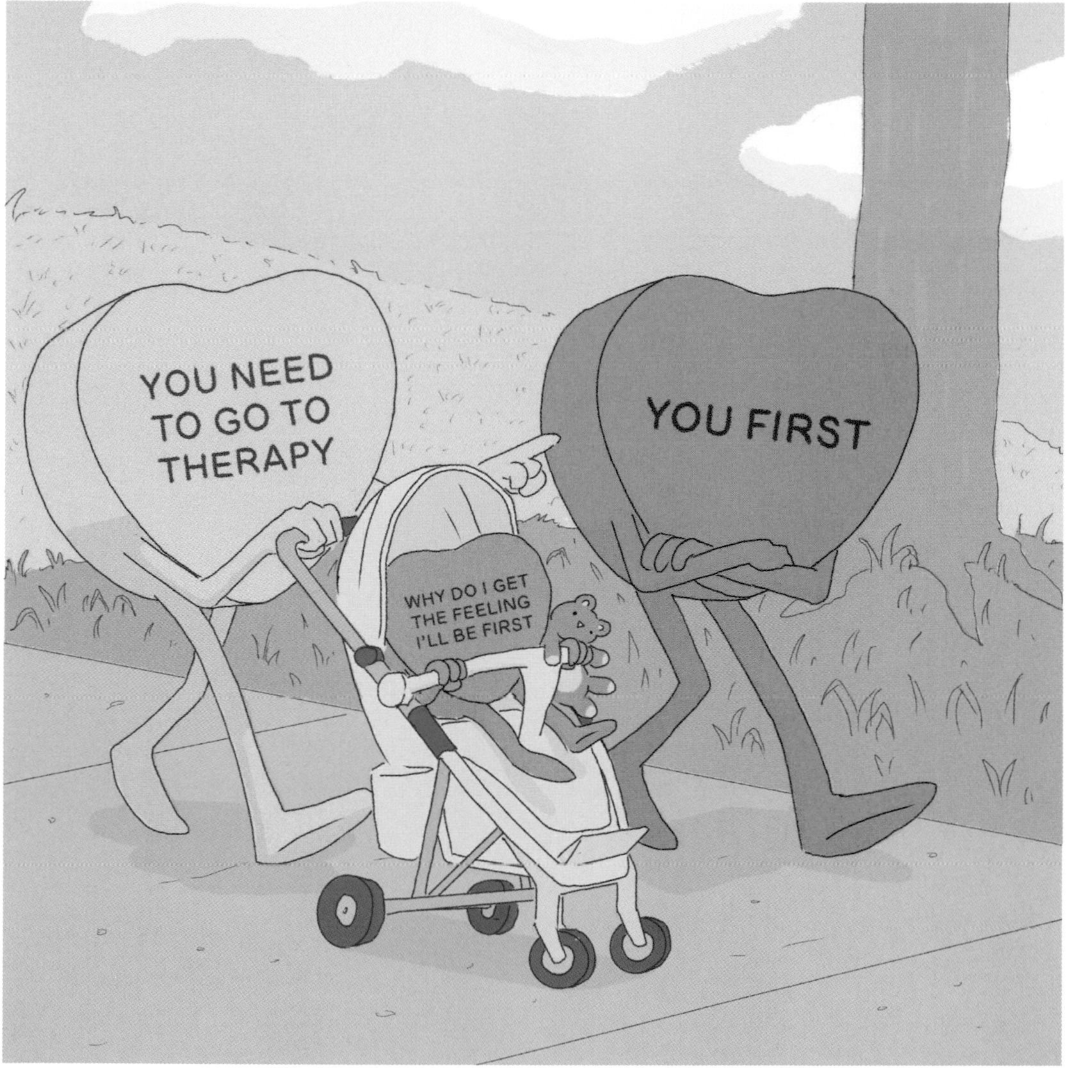
YOU NEED
TO GO TO
THERAPY
YOU FIRST
WHY DO I GET
THE FEELING
I'LL BE FIRST

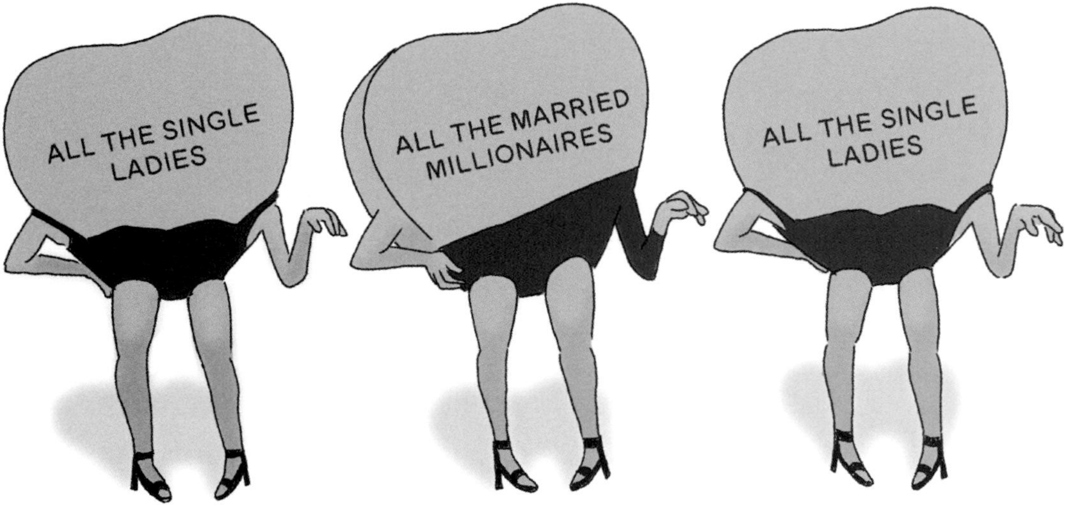
ALL THE SINGLE LADIES
ALL THE MARRIED MILLIONAIRES
ALL THE SINGLE LADIES

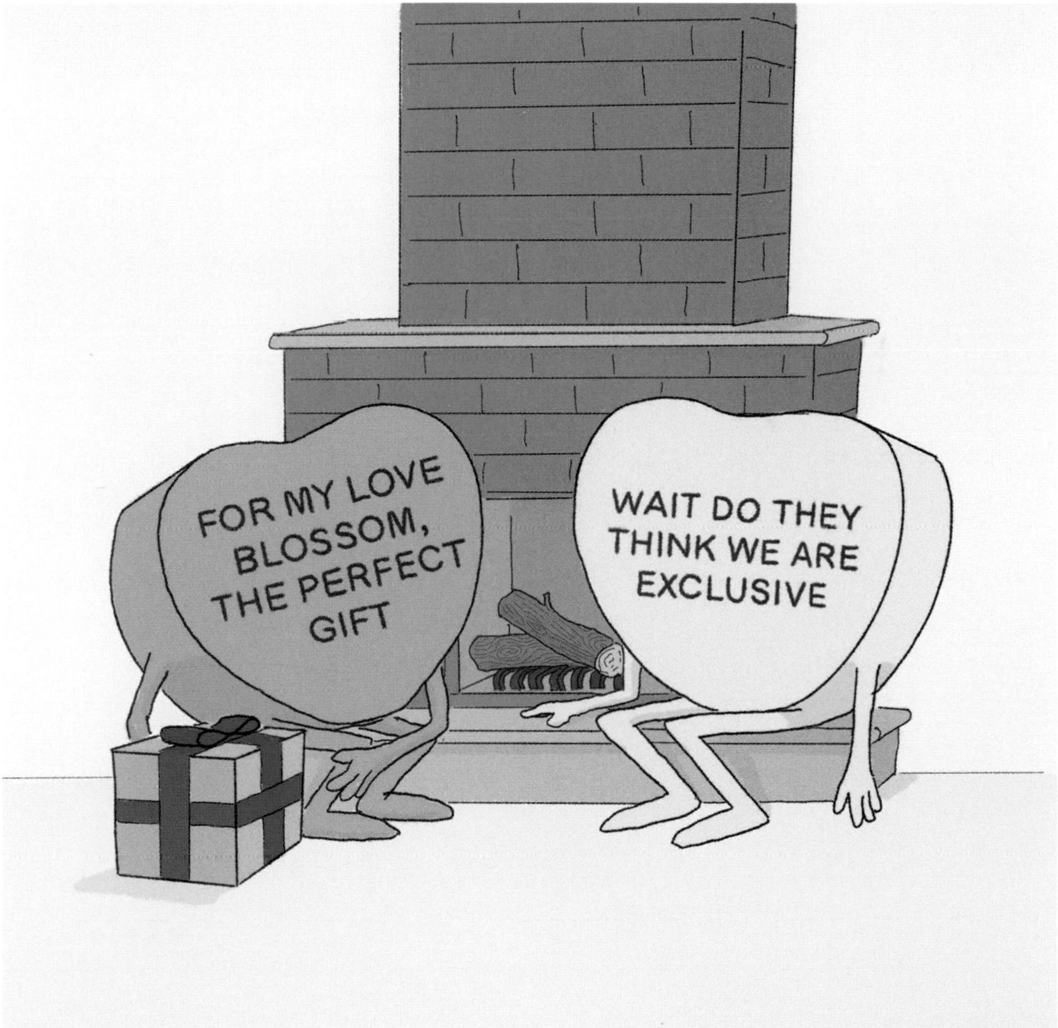
FOR MY LOVE BLOSSOM, THE PERFECT GIFT
WAIT DO THEY THINK WE ARE EXCLUSIVE

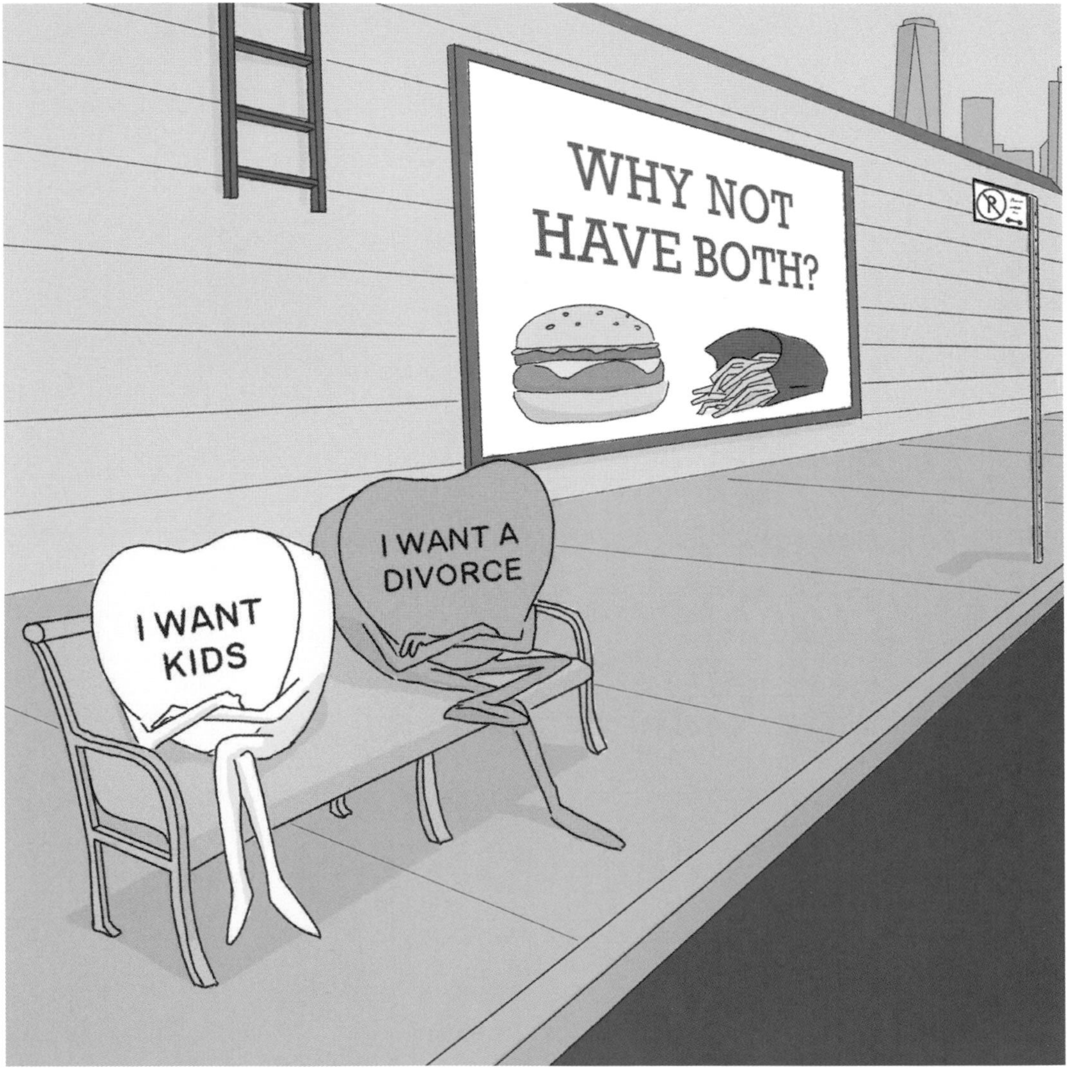
WHY NOT
HAVE BOTH?
I WANT A
DIVORCE
I WANT
KIDS

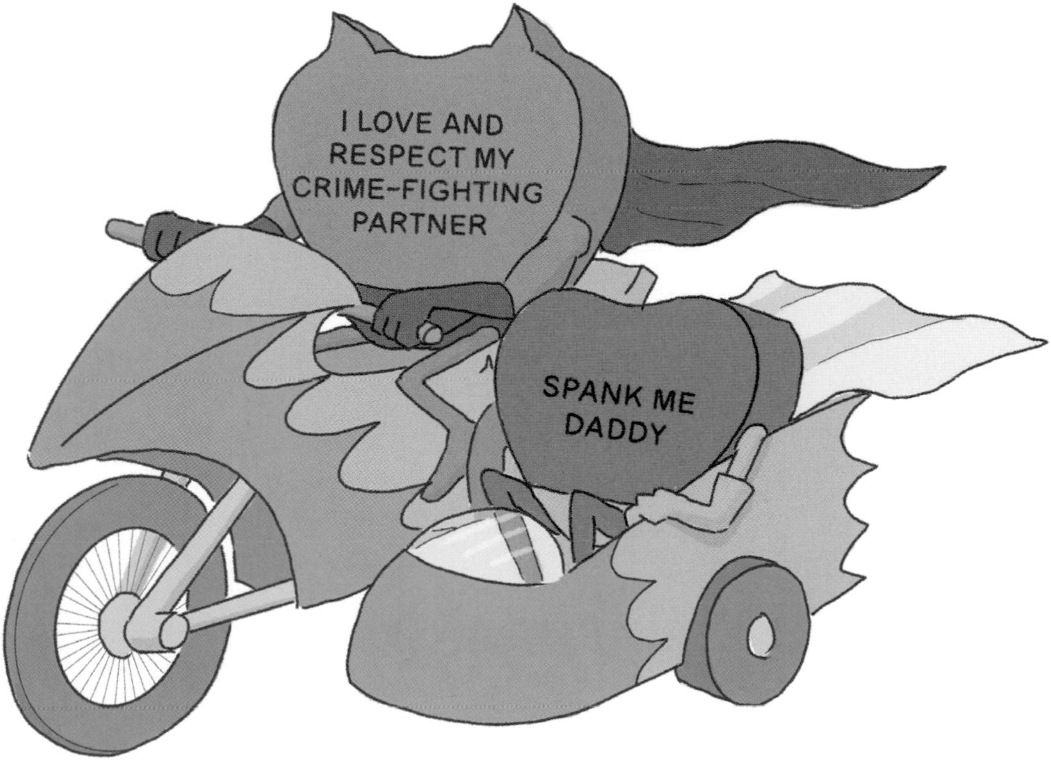
I LOVE AND RESPECT MY CRIME-FIGHTING PARTNER
SPANK ME DADDY

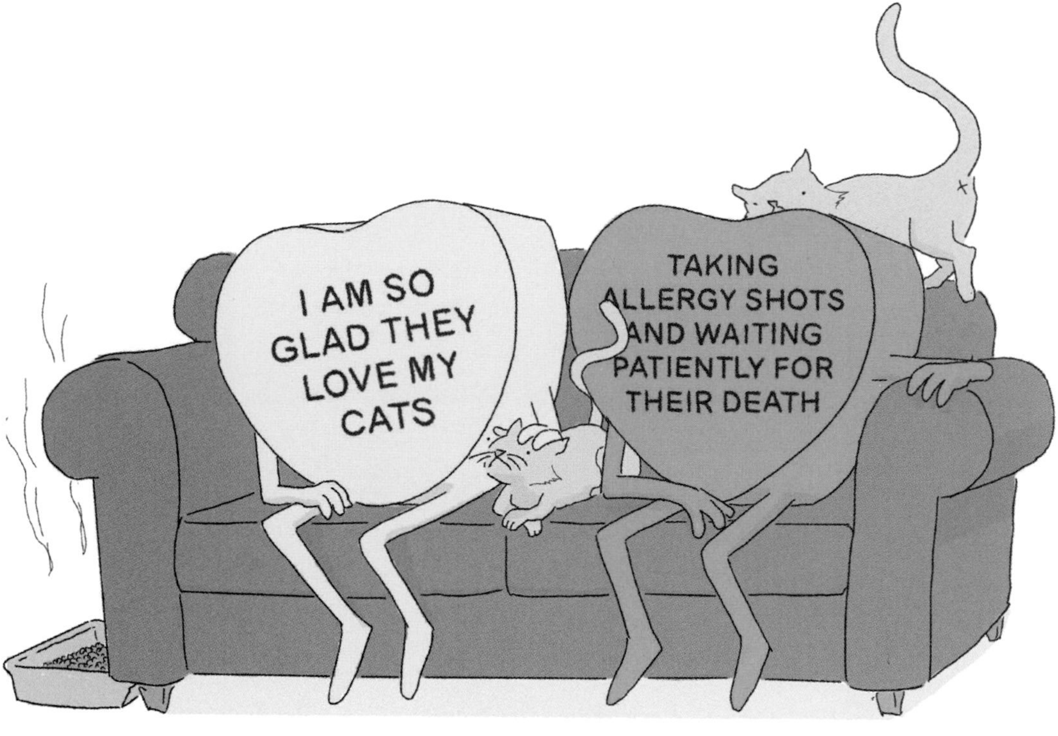
I AM SO GLAD THEY LOVE MY CATS
TAKING ALLERGY SHOTS AND WAITING PATIENTLY FOR THEIR DEATH

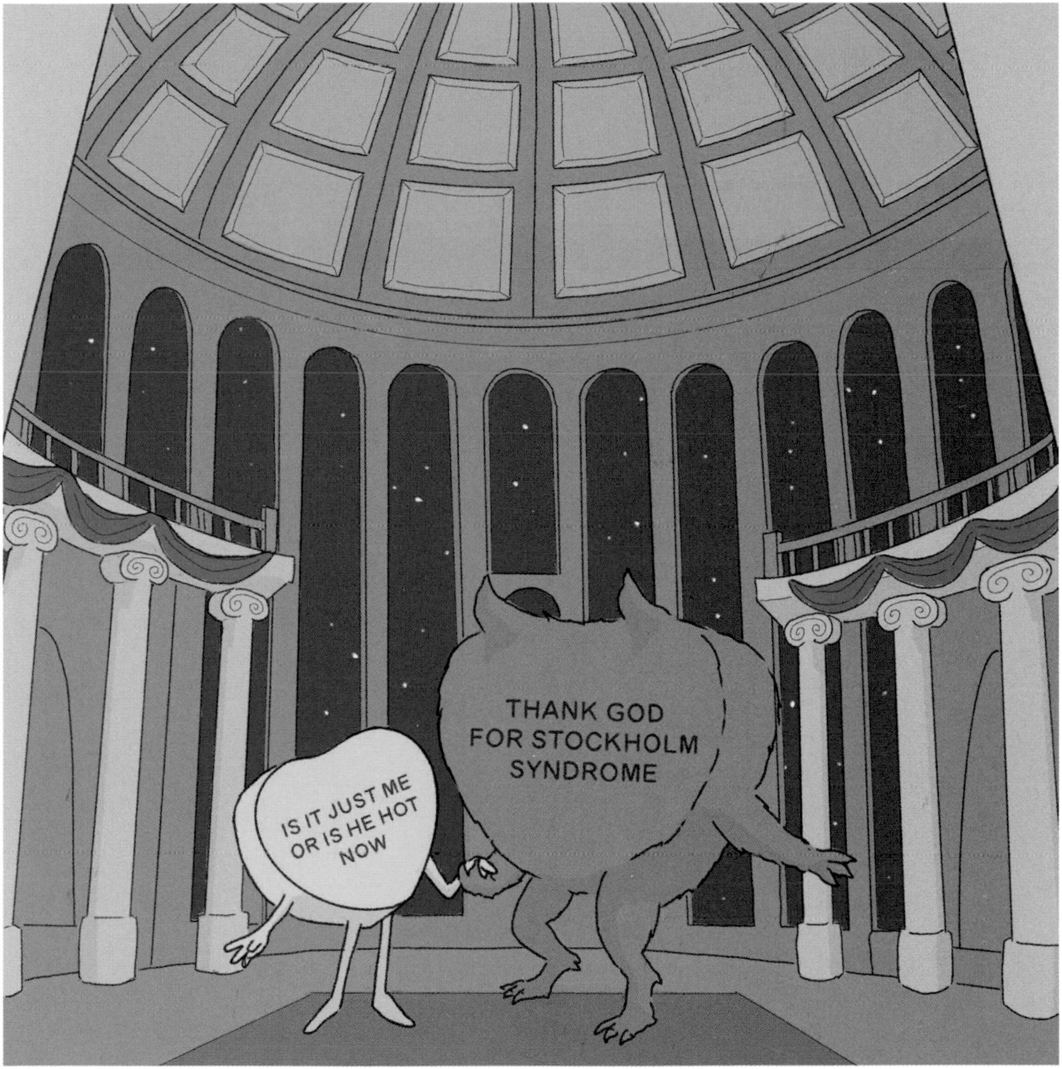
IS IT JUST ME
OR IS HE HOT
NOW
THANK GOD
FOR STOCKHOLM
SYNDROME

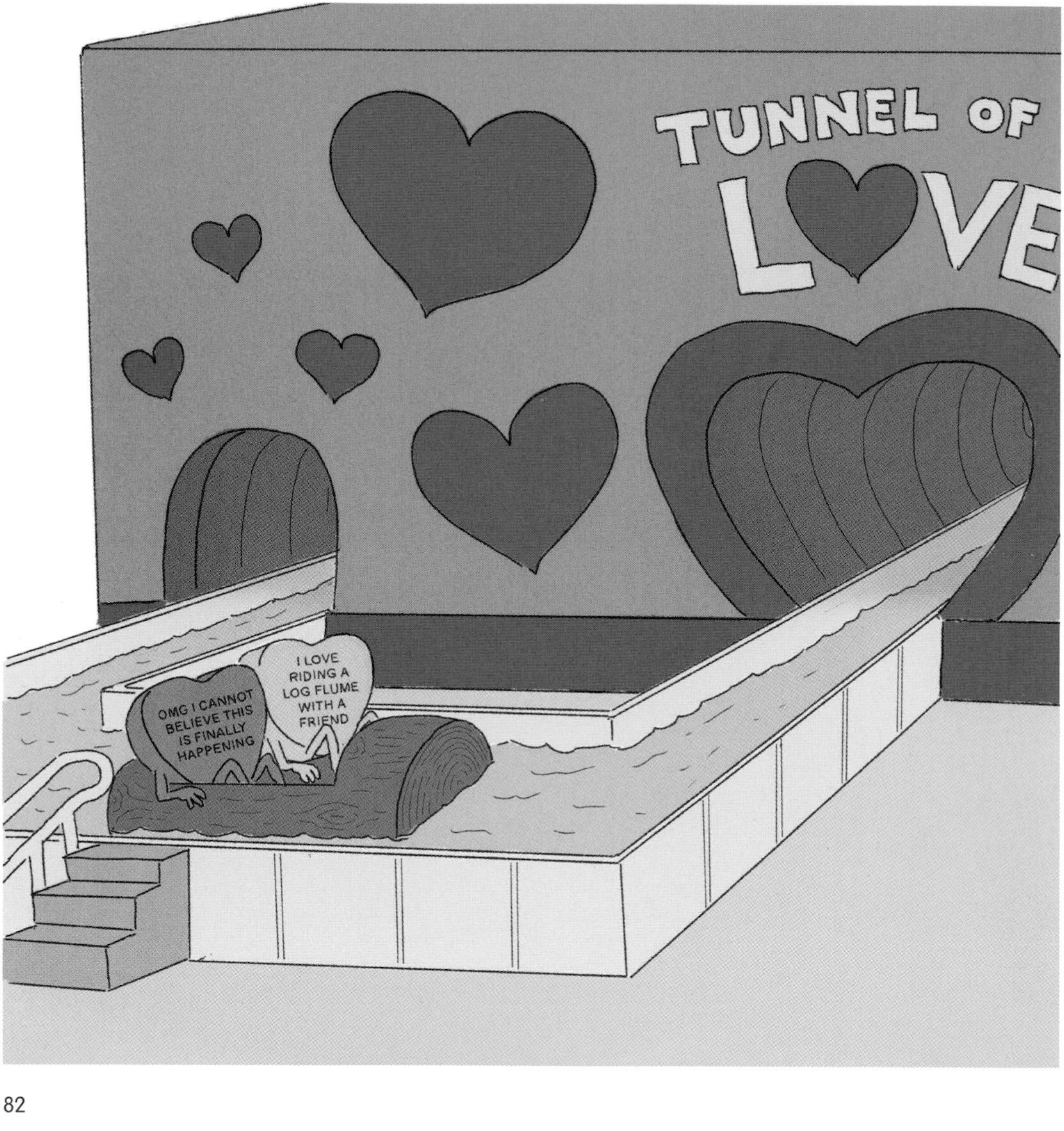
TUNNEL OF
LOVE
OMG I CANNOT BELIEVE THIS IS FINALLY HAPPENING
I LOVE RIDING A LOG FLUME WITH A FRIEND

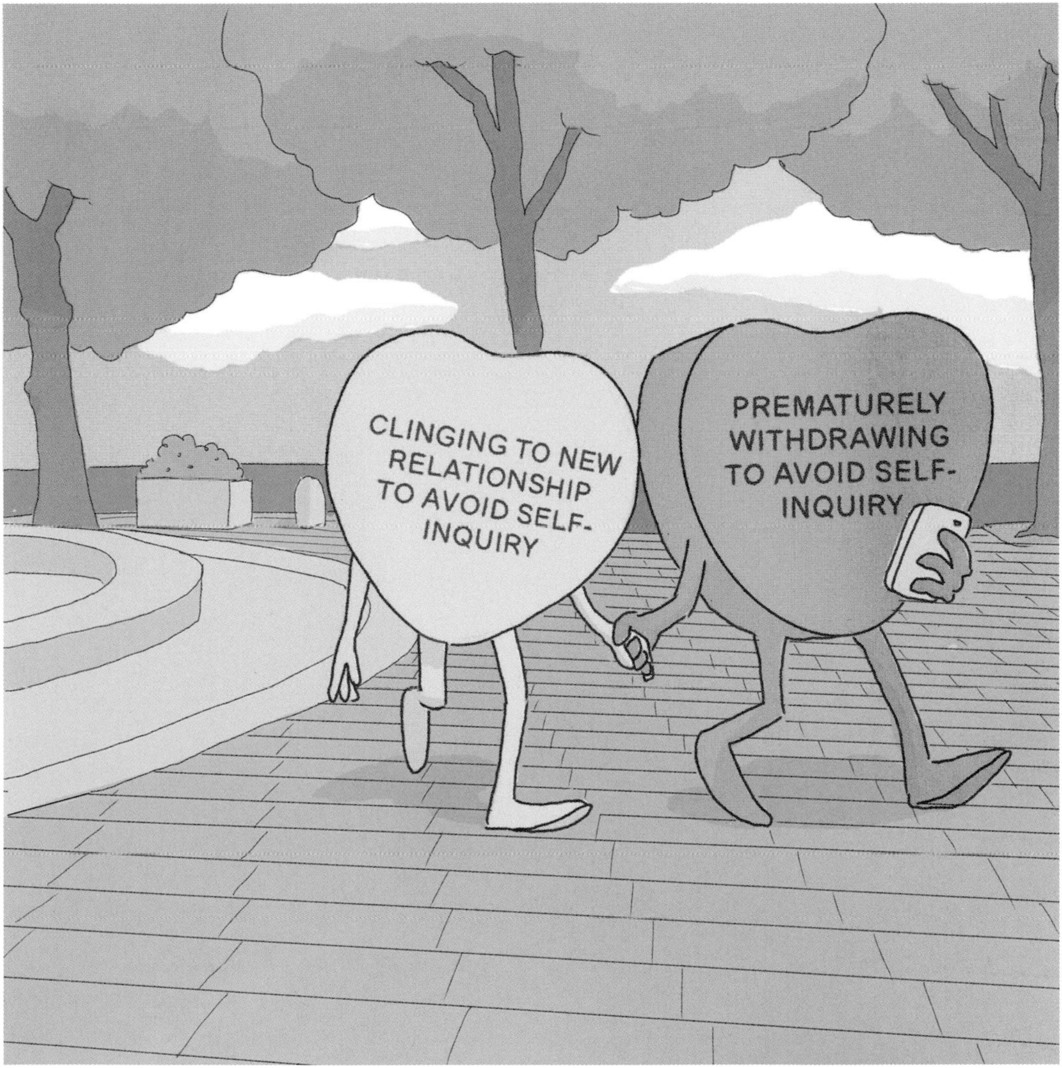
CLINGING TO NEW RELATIONSHIP TO AVOID SELF-INQUIRY
PREMATURELY WITHDRAWING TO AVOID SELF-INQUIRY

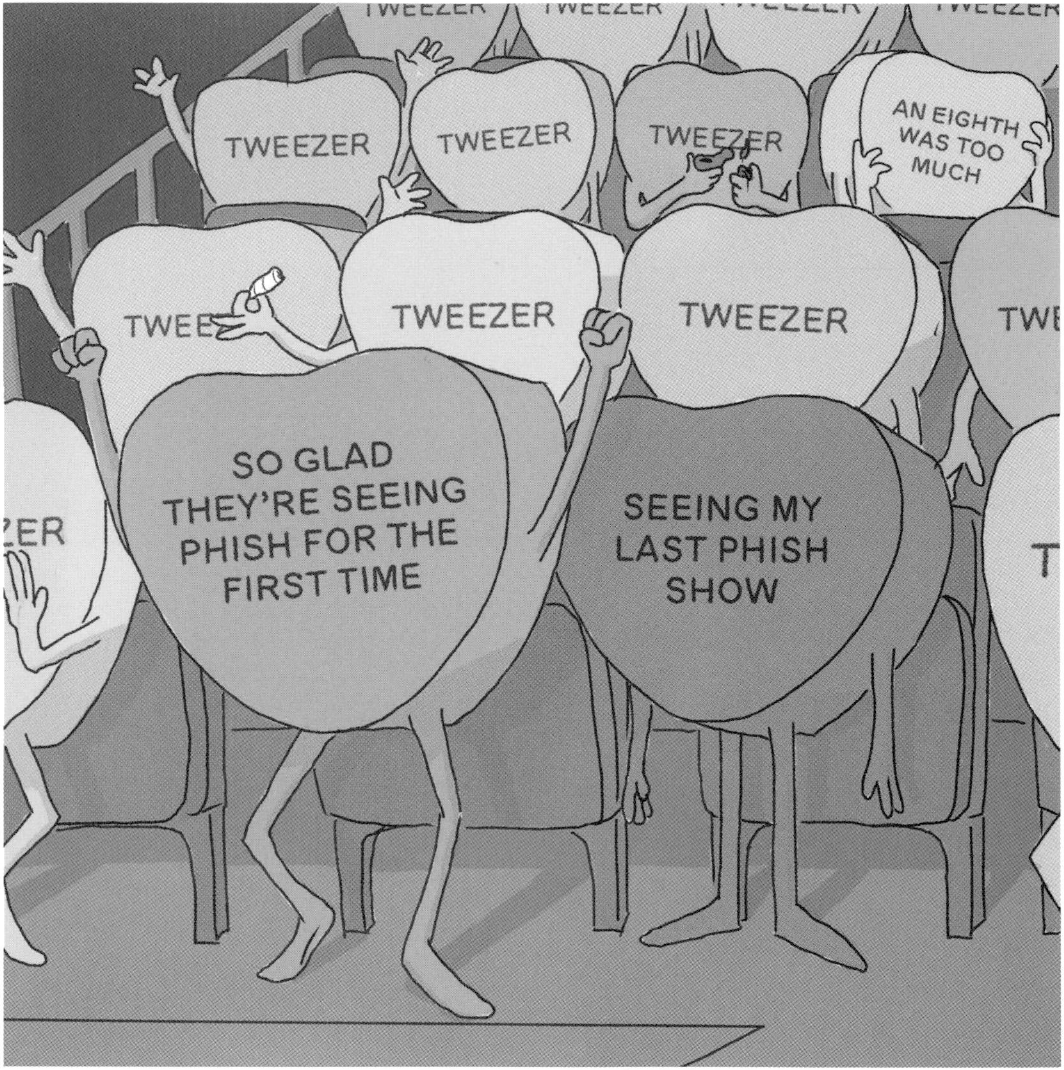
TWEEZER
TWEEZER
TWEEZER
AN EIGHTH WAS TOO MUCH
TWEEZER
TWEEZER
SO GLAD THEY'RE SEEING PHISH FOR THE FIRST TIME
SEEING MY LAST PHISH SHOW

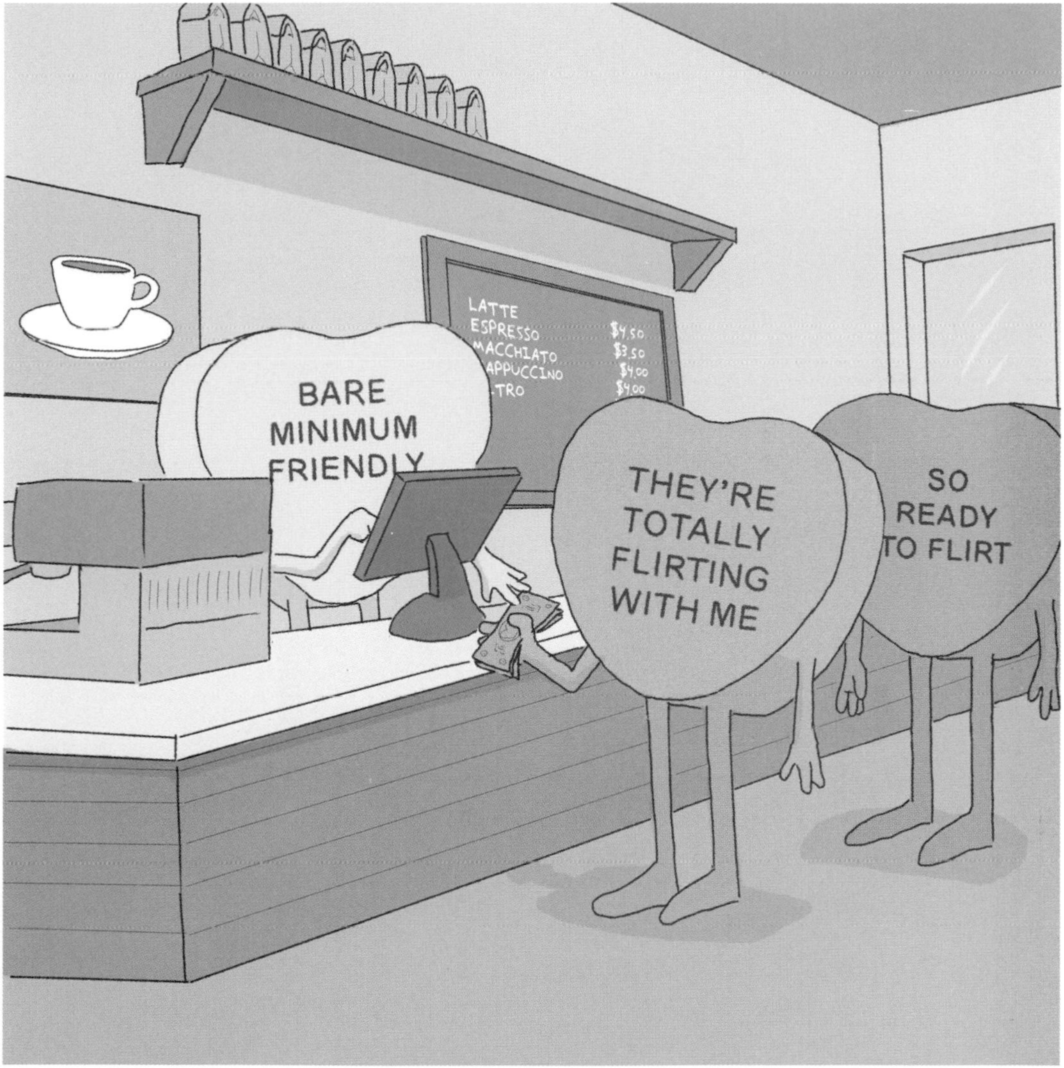
LATTE
ESPRESSO $4.50
$3.50
$4.00
$4.00
BARE MINIMUM FRIENDLY
THEY'RE TOTALLY FLIRTING WITH ME
SO READY TO FLIRT

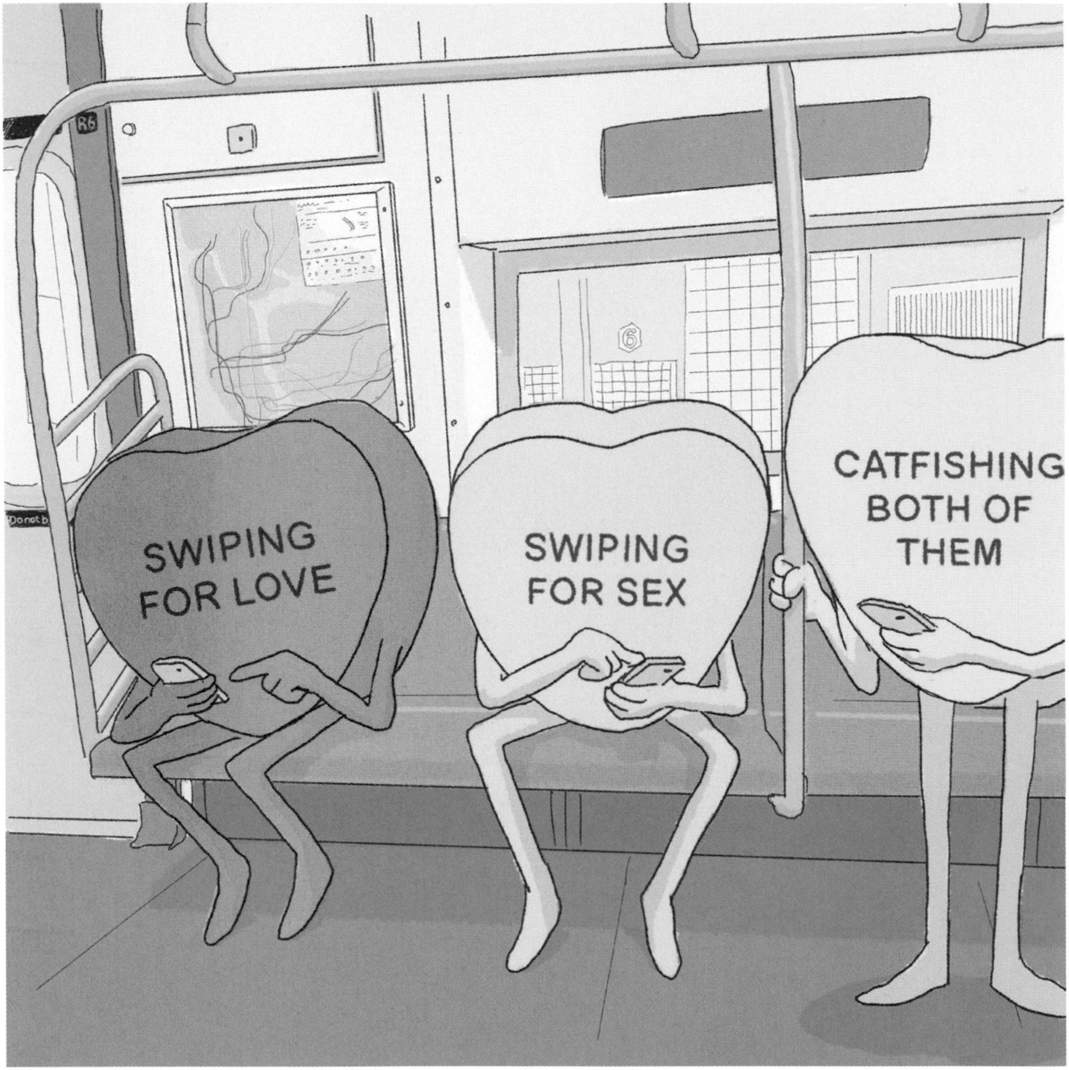
SWIPING FOR LOVE
SWIPING FOR SEX
CATFISHING BOTH OF THEM

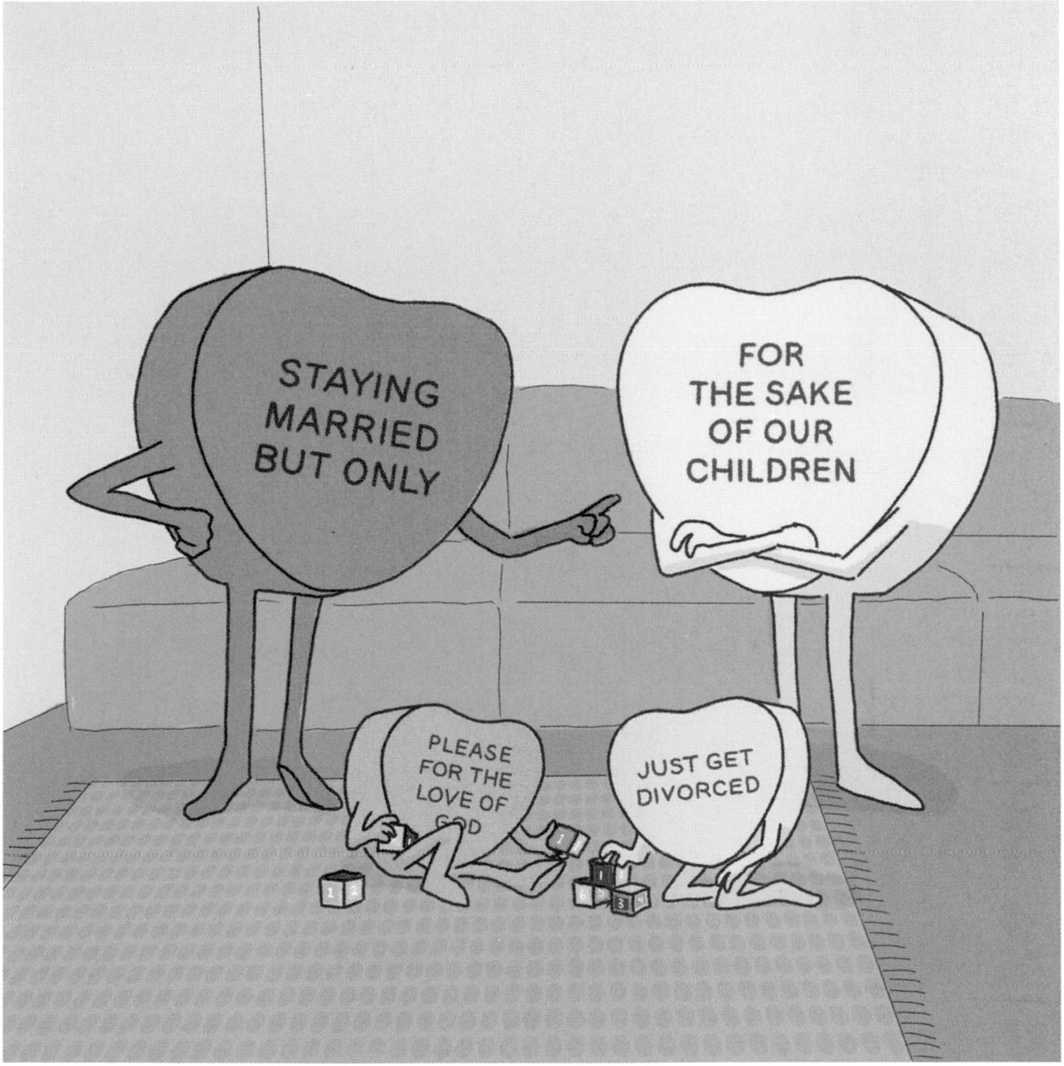
STAYING MARRIED BUT ONLY
FOR THE SAKE OF OUR CHILDREN
PLEASE FOR THE LOVE OF GOD
JUST GET DIVORCED

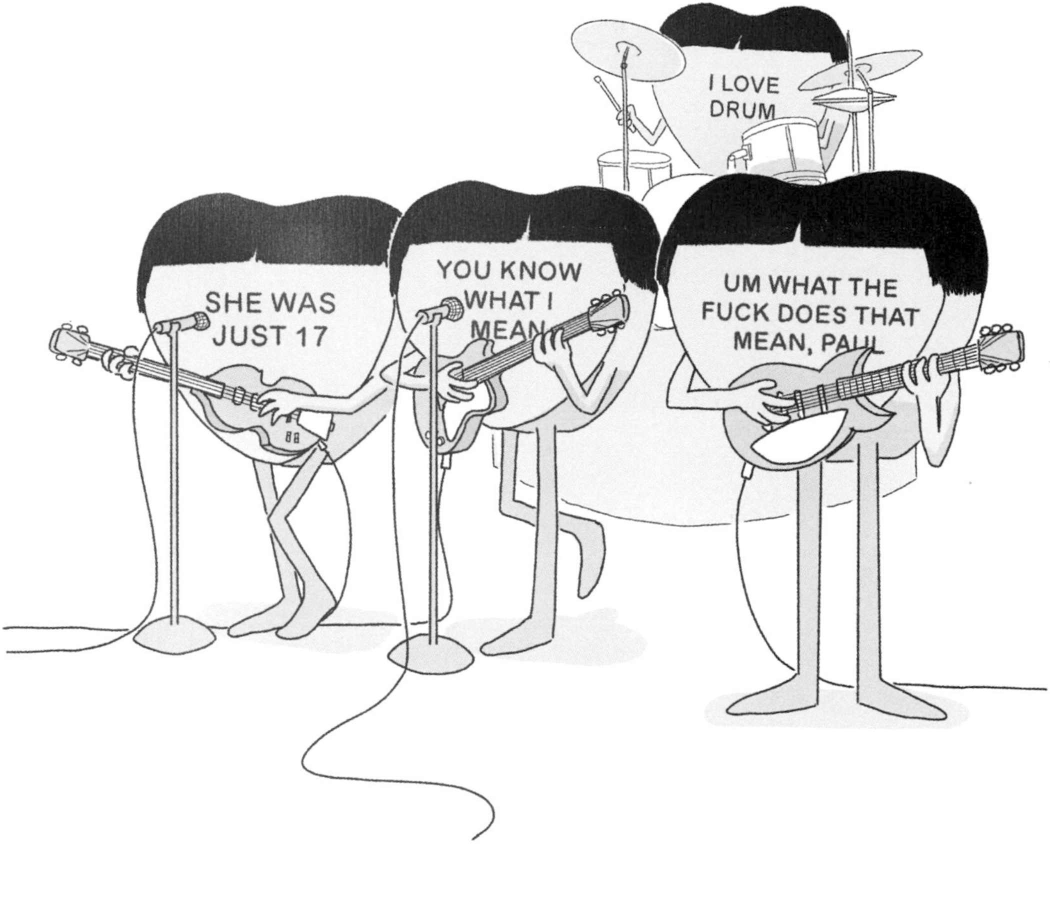
I LOVE DRUM
SHE WAS JUST 17
YOU KNOW WHAT I MEAN
UM WHAT THE FUCK DOES THAT MEAN, PAUL

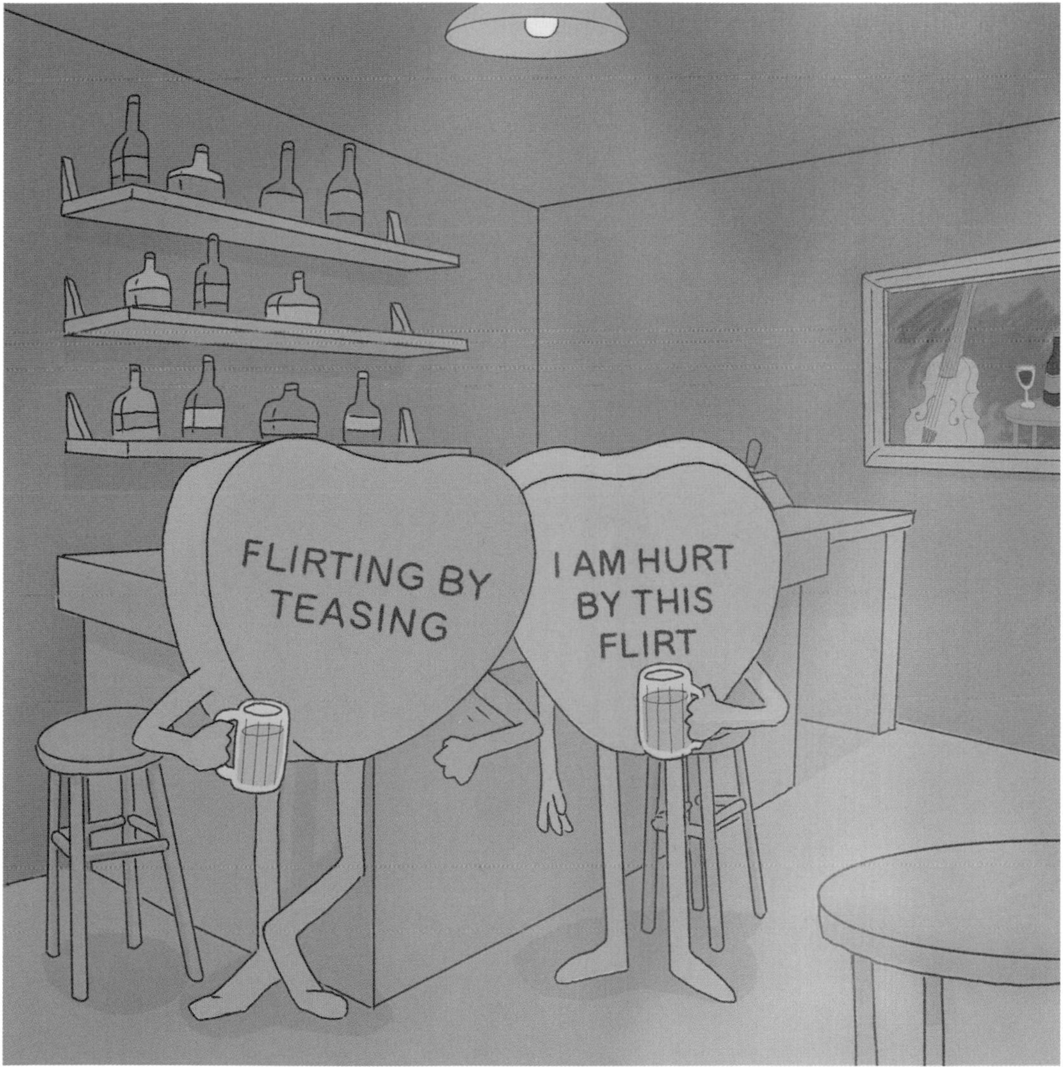
FLIRTING BY TEASING
I AM HURT BY THIS FLIRT

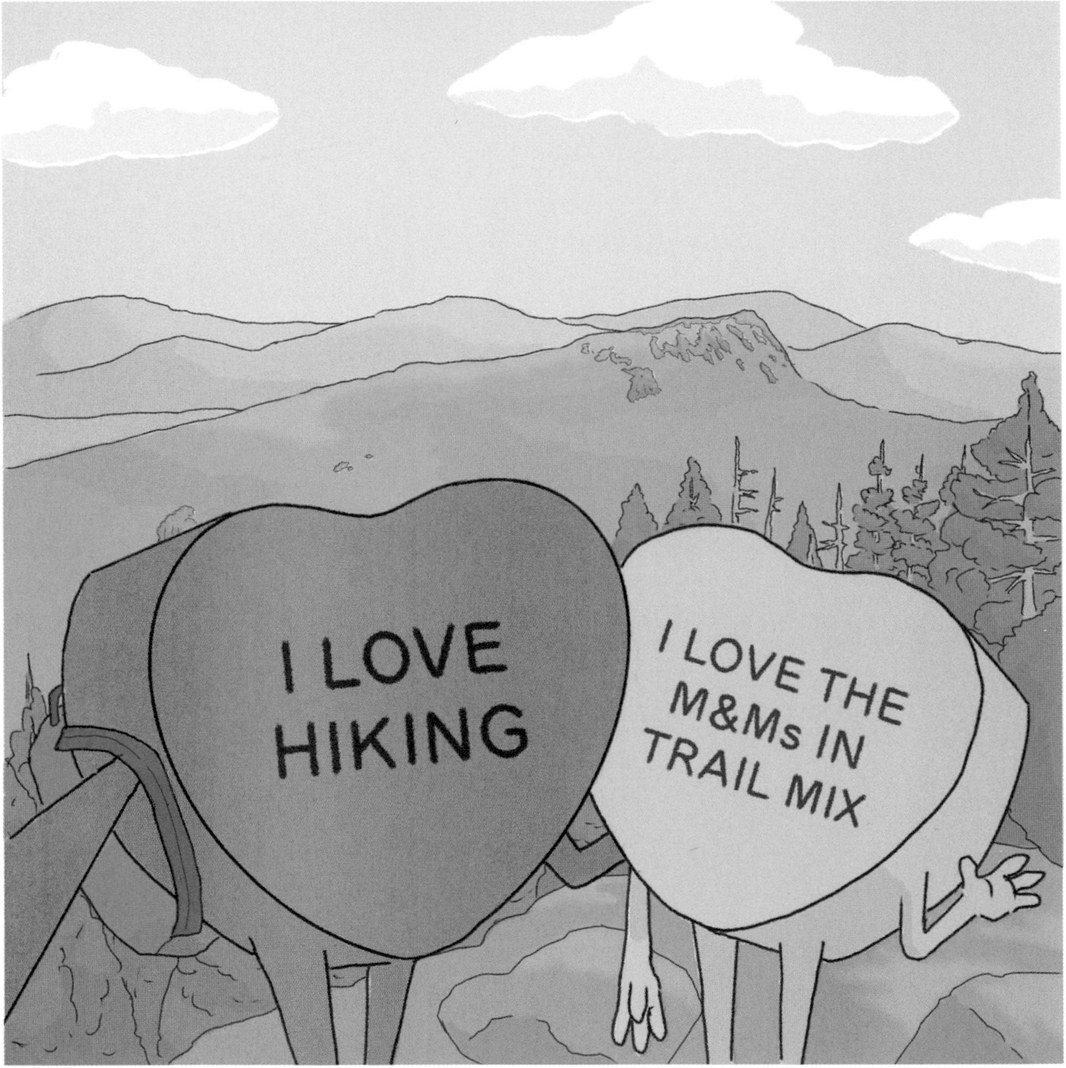
I LOVE HIKING
I LOVE THE M&Ms IN TRAIL MIX

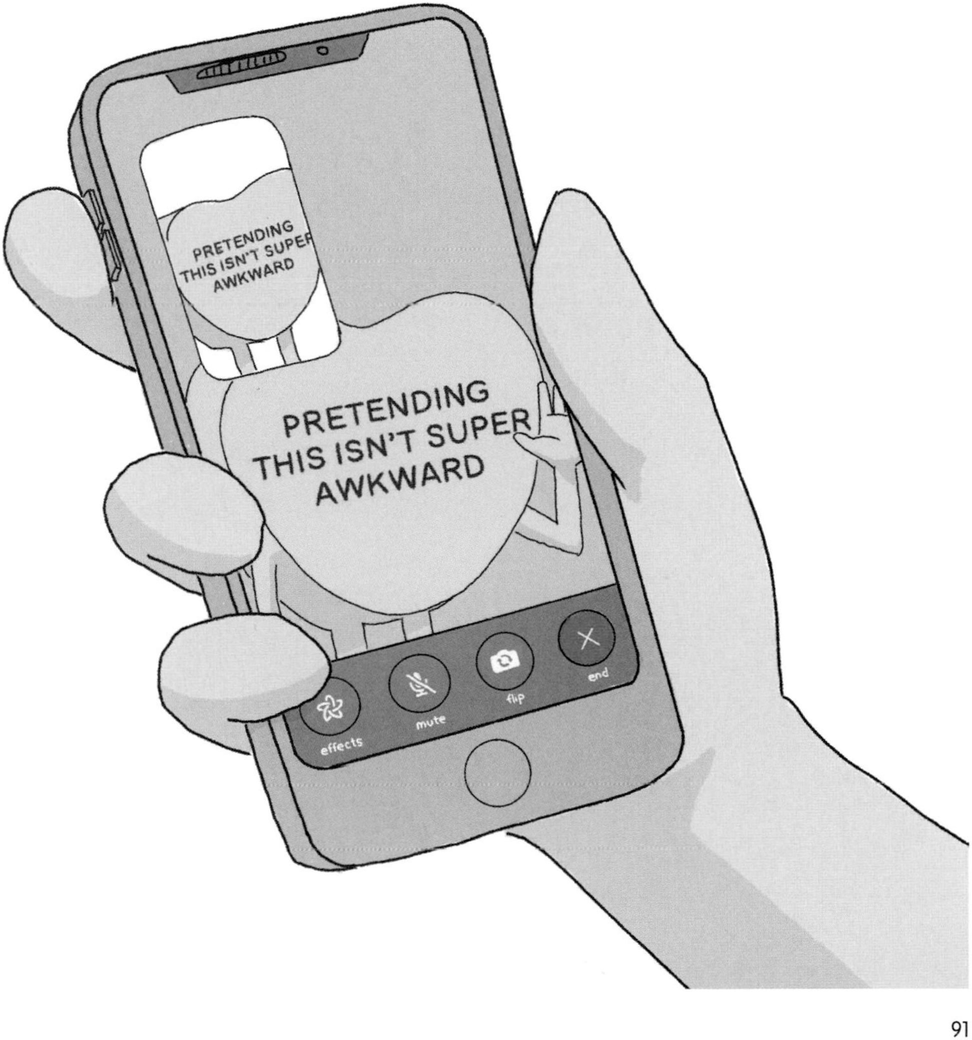
PRETENDING
THIS ISN'T SUPER
AWKWARD
PRETENDING
THIS ISN'T SUPER
AWKWARD
effects
mute
flip
end

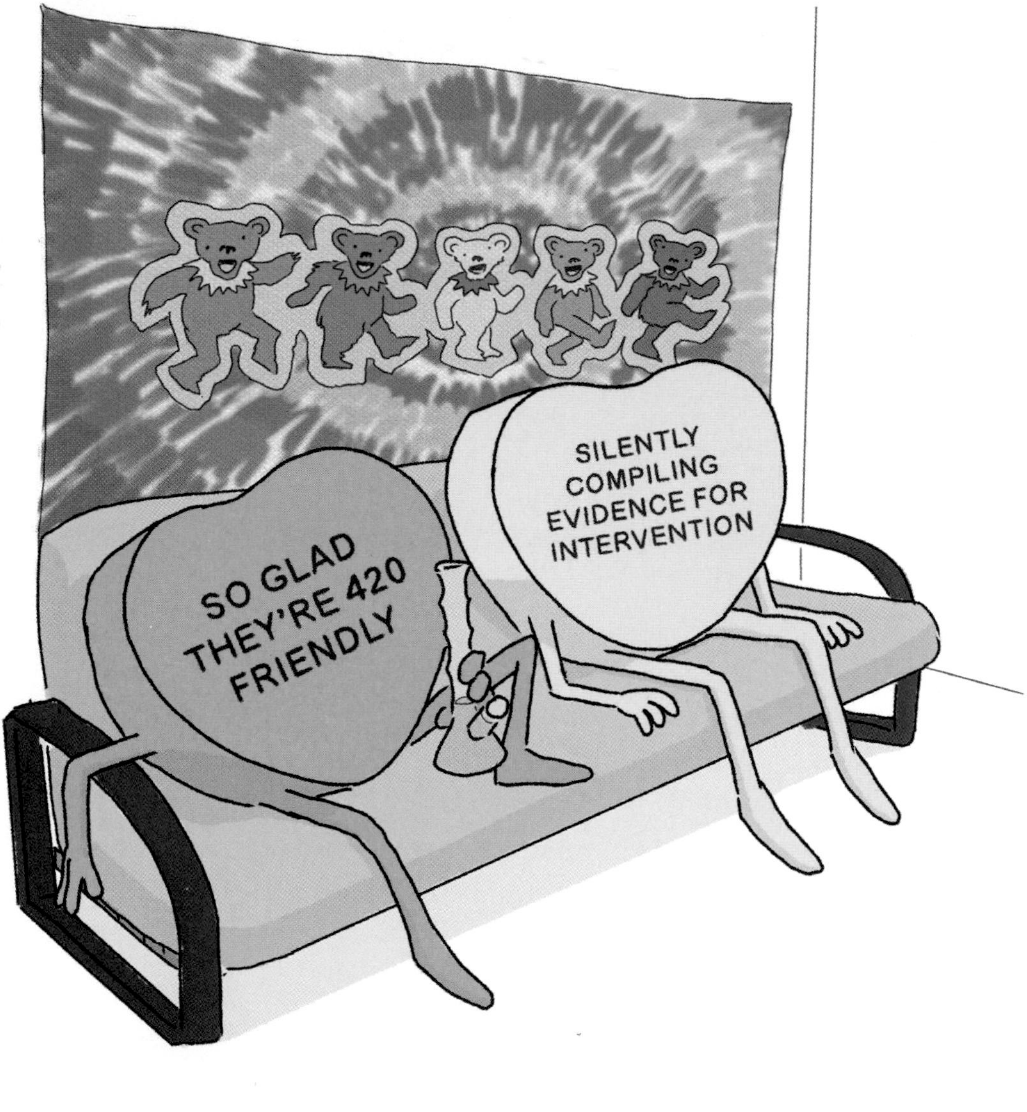
SO GLAD THEY'RE 420 FRIENDLY
SILENTLY COMPILING EVIDENCE FOR INTERVENTION

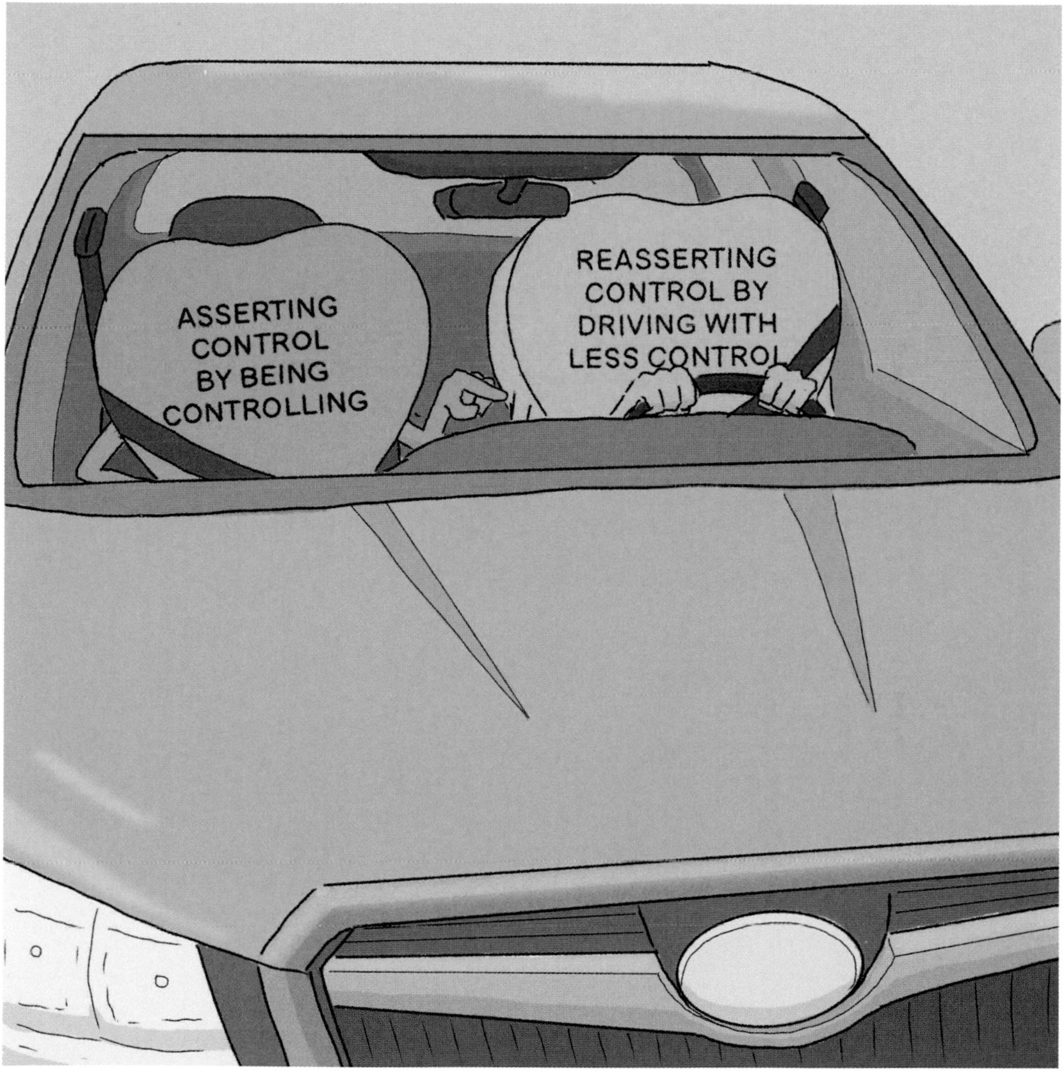
ASSERTING CONTROL BY BEING CONTROLLING
REASSERTING CONTROL BY DRIVING WITH LESS CONTROL

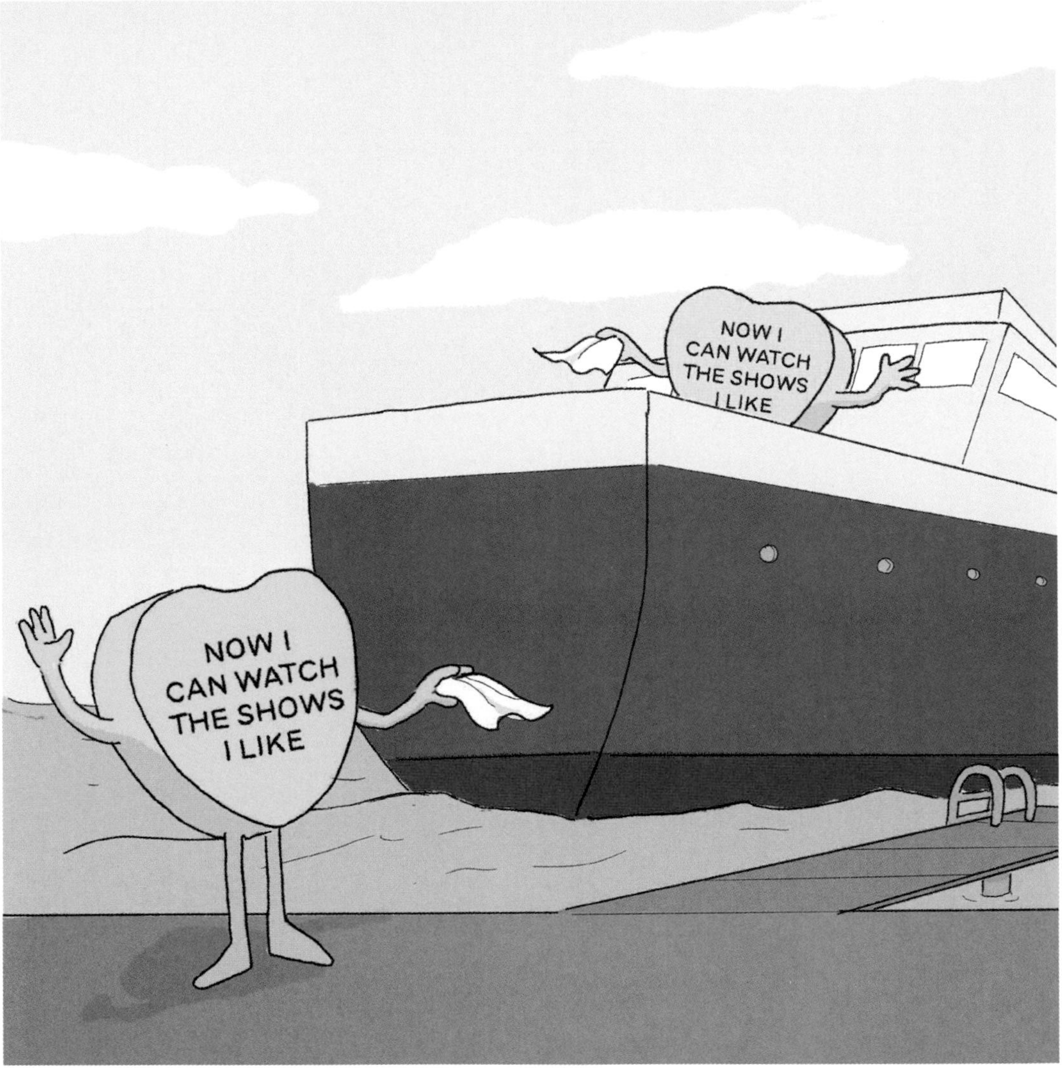
NOW I
CAN WATCH
THE SHOWS
I LIKE
NOW I
CAN WATCH
THE SHOWS
I LIKE

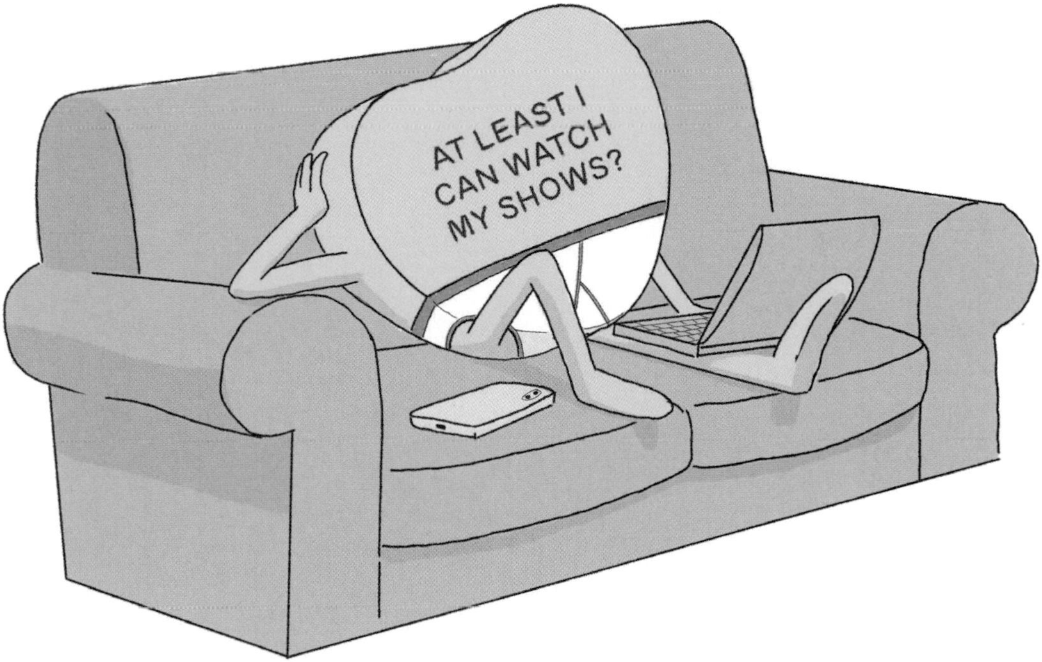
AT LEAST I
CAN WATCH
MY SHOWS?

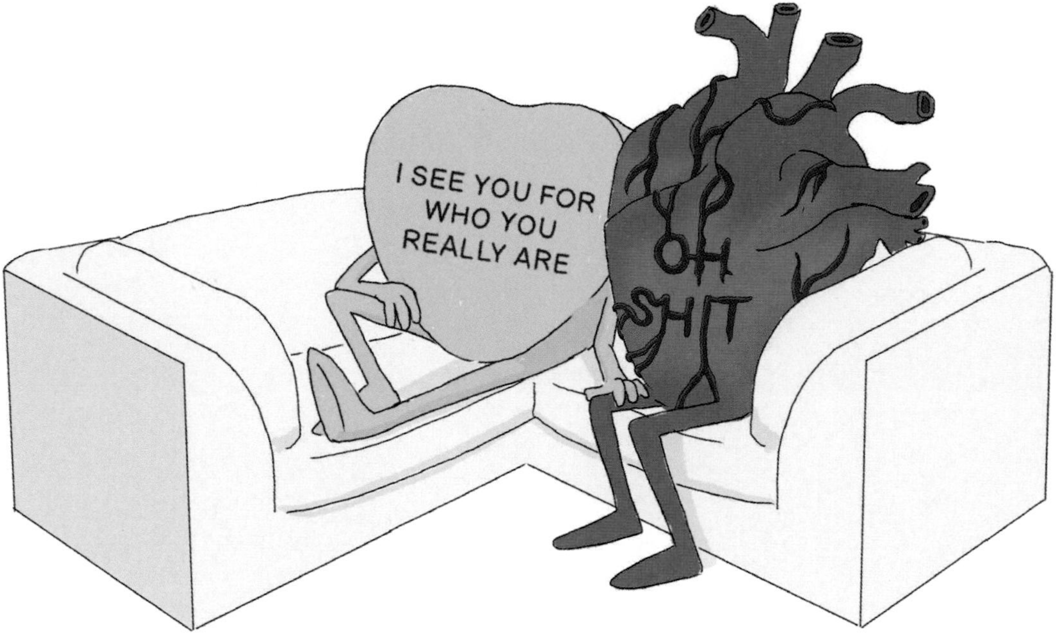
I SEE YOU FOR
WHO YOU
REALLY ARE
OH
SHIT

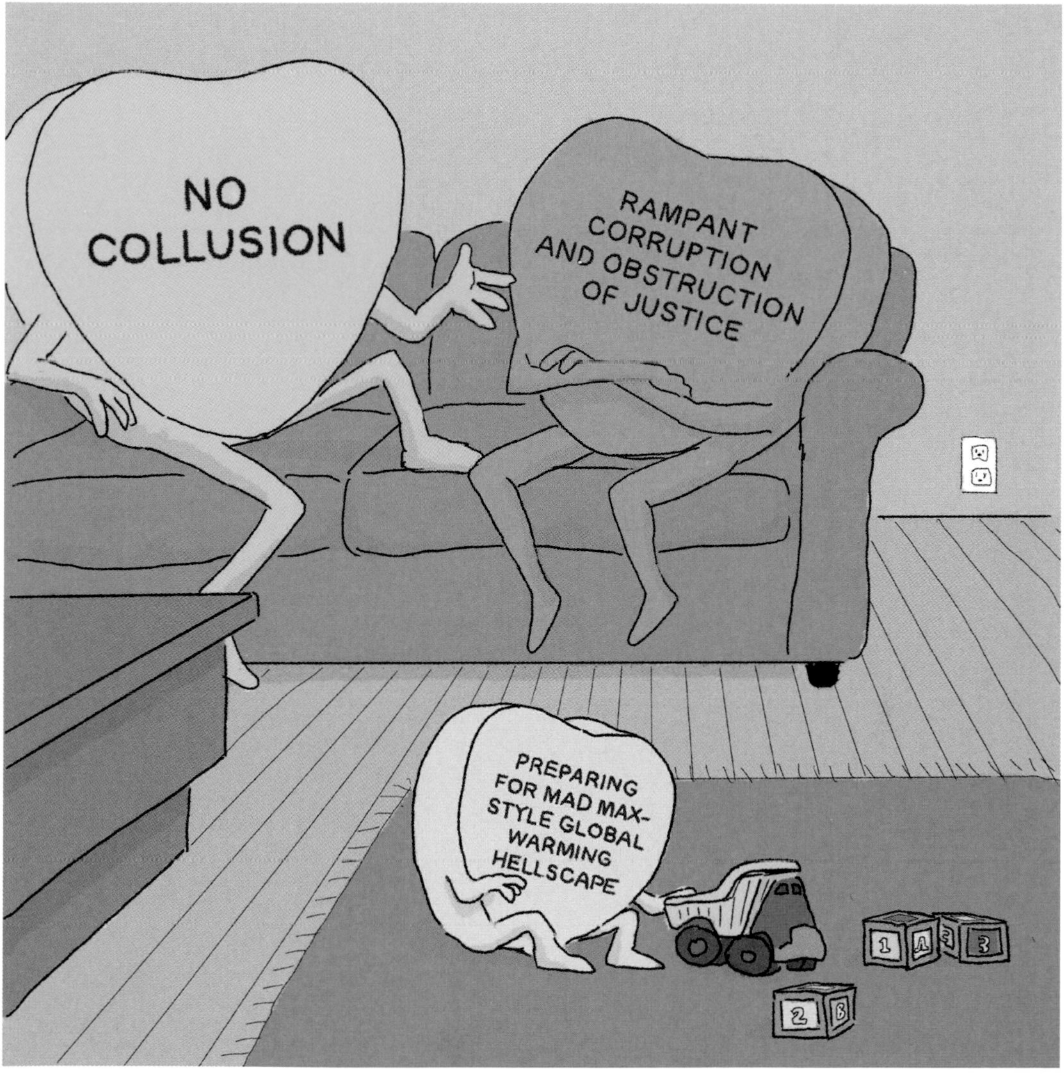
NO
COLLUSION
RAMPANT
CORRUPTION
AND OBSTRUCTION
OF JUSTICE
PREPARING
FOR MAD MAX-
STYLE GLOBAL
WARMING
HELLSCAPE

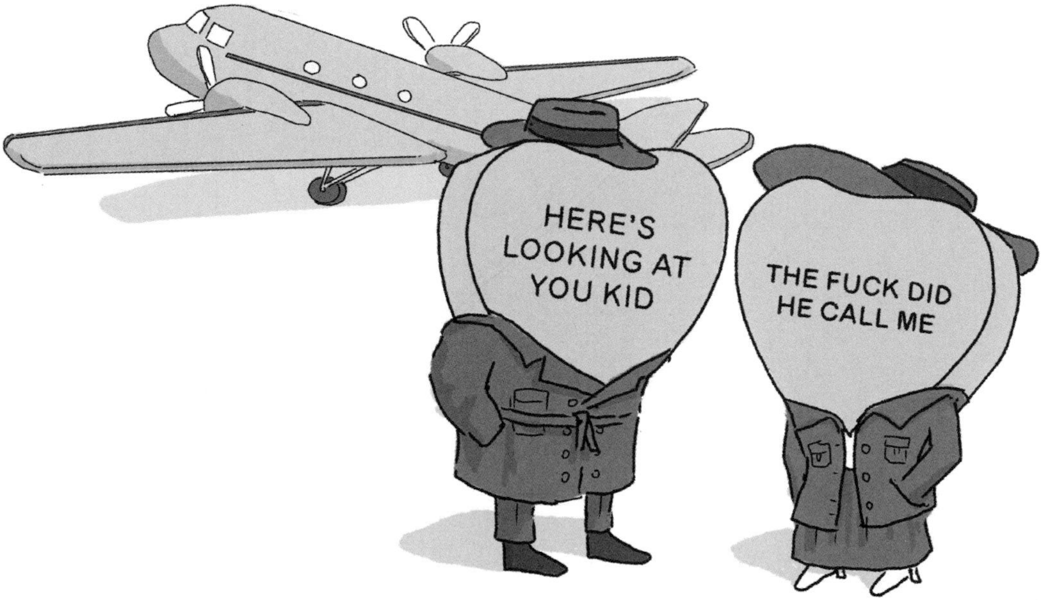
HERE'S
LOOKING AT
YOU KID
THE FUCK DID
HE CALL ME

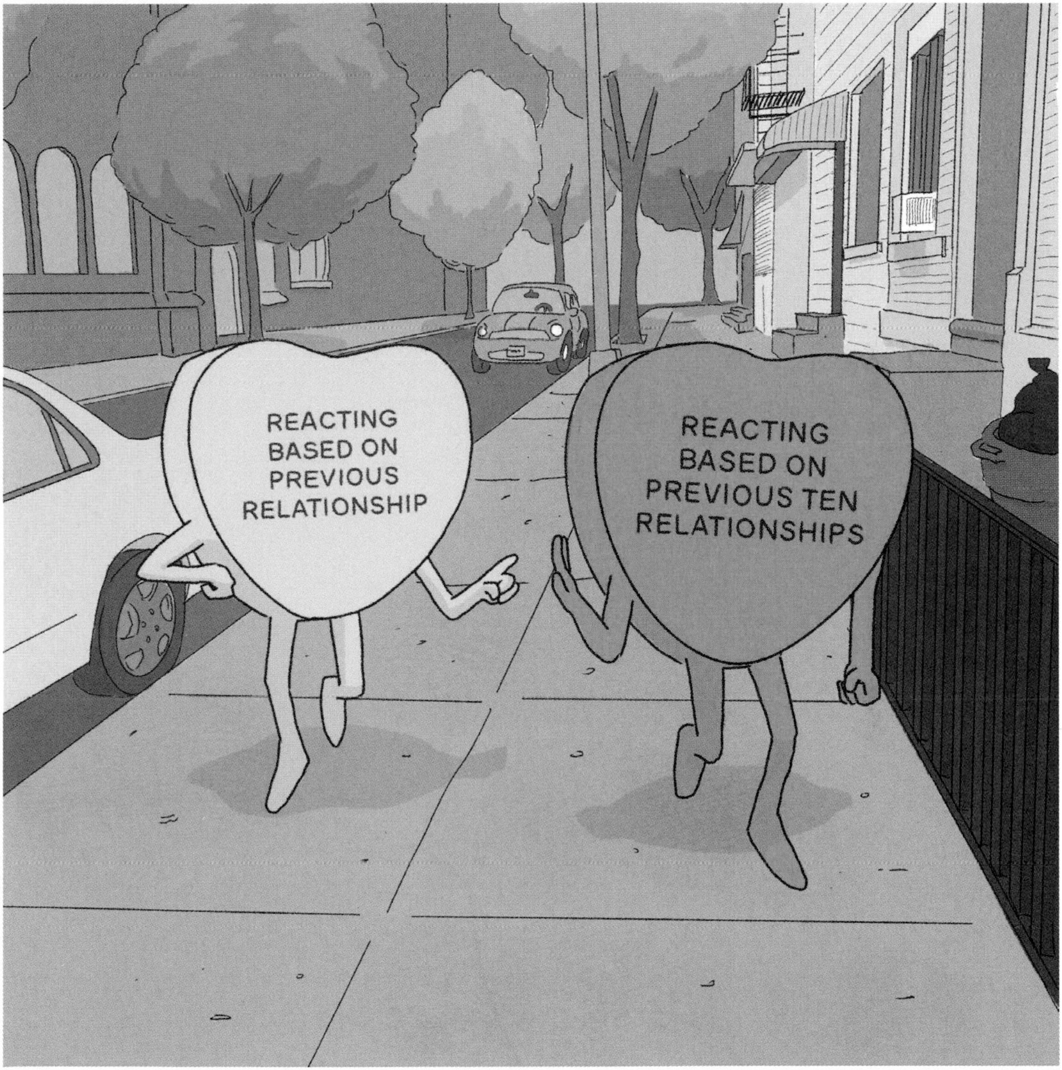
REACTING
BASED ON
PREVIOUS
RELATIONSHIP
REACTING
BASED ON
PREVIOUS TEN
RELATIONSHIPS

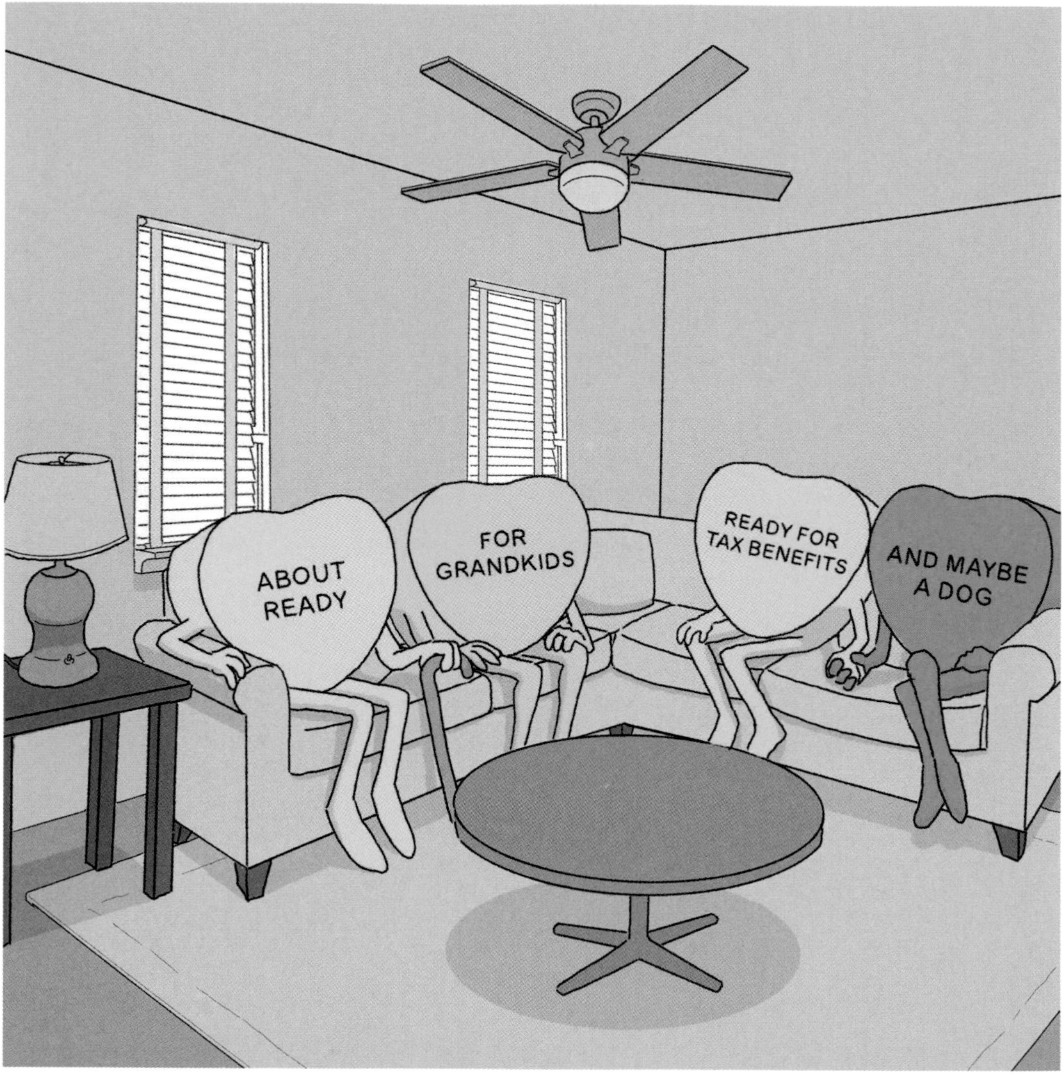
ABOUT READY
FOR GRANDKIDS
READY FOR TAX BENEFITS
AND MAYBE A DOG

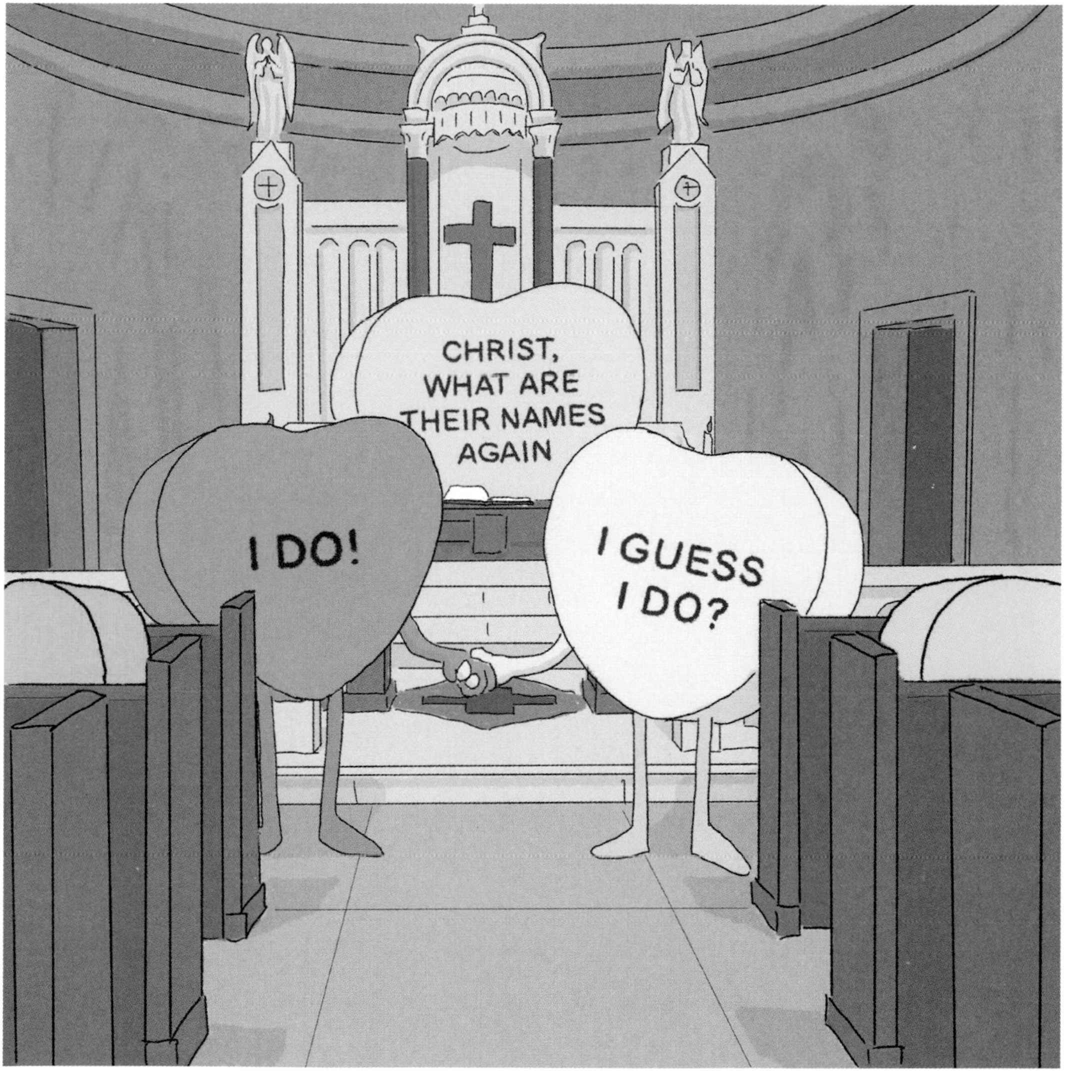
CHRIST,
WHAT ARE
THEIR NAMES
AGAIN
I DO!
I GUESS
I DO?

ACKNOWLEDGMENTS

It's something that's always said, but I *truly* couldn't have made this collection without help from my friends and family, many of whom served as collaborators, creative springboards, and informal editors.

First and foremost, an endless amount of gratitude to my parents, who encouraged and fanned the flames of my comics obsession as a kid. I was also lucky enough to have them as real-time creative consultants for comics: Much of *Candy Hearts* came together while I was quarantined with them in Richmond, Virginia, in the early stages of the pandemic. I remain endlessly thankful for their love and support, which allowed me to flourish and become a whole new kind of messed up that they never could have predicted. I love you both from the bottom of my confectionary heart.

To my best friend Dan Kirkwood, who served as an informal editor for nearly all of the comics in this book. Our mutual love for *The Far Side* and *Calvin and Hobbes* has always given us common ground, but it's a rare thing to find a friend and collaborator who can challenge your work to be better without constantly pissing you off. Somehow, he does it. It's a special kind of friendship magic — I don't take it for granted.

The final third of the book came together while living in a quarantine pod in the woods with several close friends in Maine. To my best pal Billy Libby, who served as full-time pandemic emotional support and cocreator/editor of too many comics to list. It is thanks solely to him that you got to learn more about Batman and Robin's kinky inner life in the pages of this book. And to my dear friends Alli Rodgers and Alex Mannix, both of whom provided fantastic concepts, helpful changes, and better punchlines for many of the comics. Because of this group of amazing people, I will feel eternally grateful and guilty for having a productive, social, and happy summer in 2020, when such things were . . . seemingly impossible.

To my sister, Julia Siegel Breton, and my brother-in-law, Andrew (Gumby) Breton, who have been cheerleaders for all my creative work, in all its forms. To my bandmates, Ben Thornewill and Jesse Kristin, who have supported my new life in comics even when it resulted in an extremely distracted bandmate. To my friend Jessie Willen, whom I can always count on for killer ideas and feedback.

To my followers who cheered me on along this journey, especially to those who supported my Patreon and gave me a glimmer of hope that it wasn't crazy to try to pursue comics as a career.

To my agent, Lisa Leshne, at the Leshne Agency, who believed in my ability to get a book published long before it was reasonable to think so. And to my badass editor, Lucas Wetzel, who also became a full-on creative collaborator and joke-enhancer as the project wore on, amid trading live Grateful Dead recommendations. I can't wait to work on another project together.

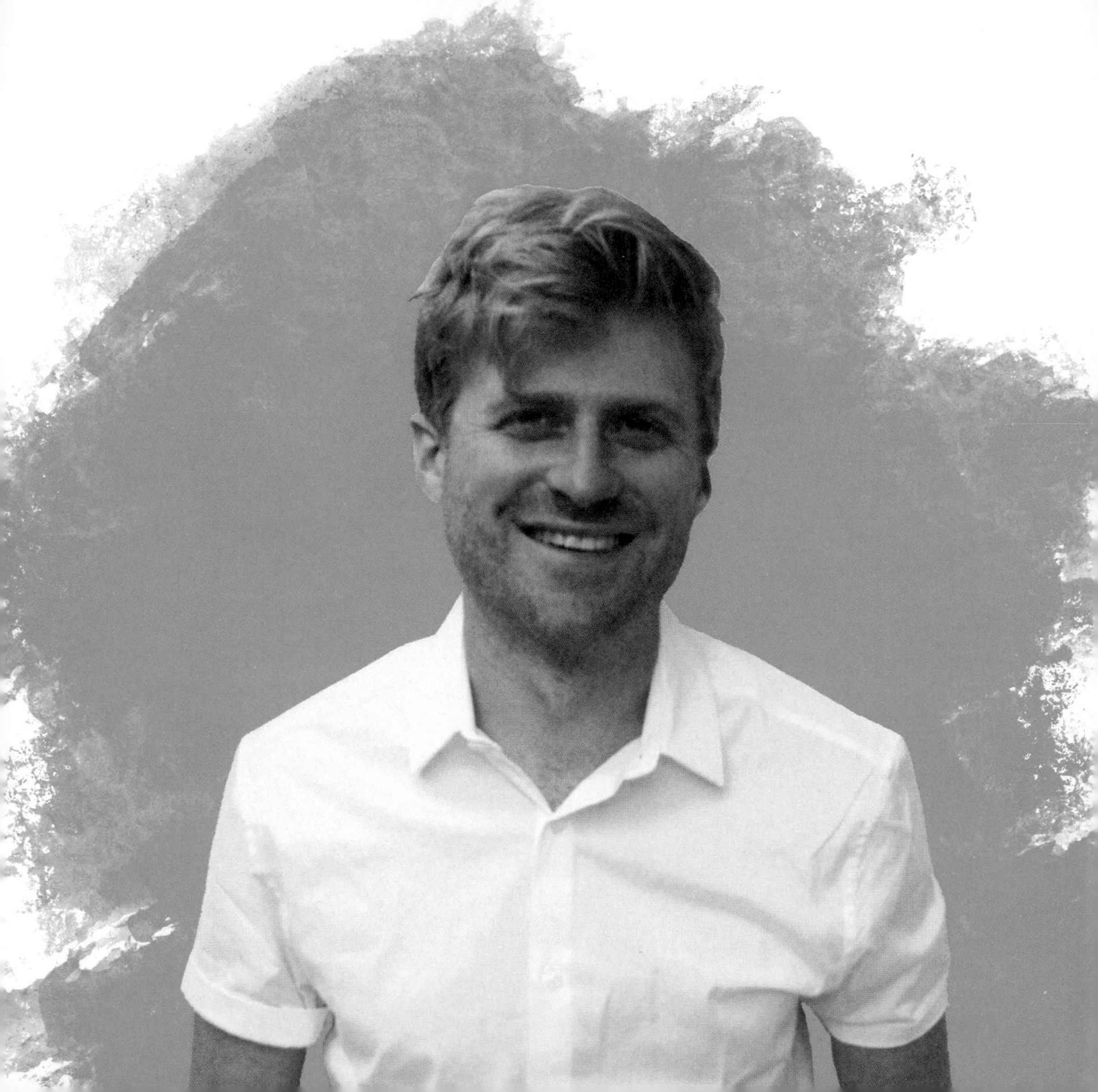

ABOUT THE AUTHOR

Tommy Siegel created the Candy Hearts series during his 500-day drawing challenge, when he drew and posted a new comic on social media for 500 days in a row, earning a global fanbase and shout-outs from cultural heavyweights like Ringo Starr and Alexandria Ocasio-Cortez. The resulting stack of comics, along with essays about the experience, were eventually whittled down into his debut comics collection, *I Hope This Helps*. In addition to being a cartoonist, he is a singer/songwriter/guitarist as a solo artist and in the band Jukebox the Ghost, an internationally touring pop band with a rabid cult following. In their 15-year-history as a band, they have played over 1,000 shows around the world, including appearances on late-night shows like Letterman and Conan and festivals like Bonnaroo, Outside Lands, Firefly, and Lollapalooza. Over years of touring, Tommy began drawing cartoons by request for fans of the band via social media during long drives, which eventually blossomed into a full-blown alternate life as a cartoonist. Born in Richmond, Virginia, he currently lives . . . nowhere in particular because of 2020 reasons.

Tommy Siegel's debut book collection includes 200+ pages of comics, extremely helpful guides, and tales from surviving 500 days of comics.

I HOPE THIS HELPS
COMICS AND CURES FOR 21st CENTURY PANIC
Available NOW!
Wherever books are sold
BY TOMMY SIEGEL
SIEGEL
I HOPE THIS HELPS

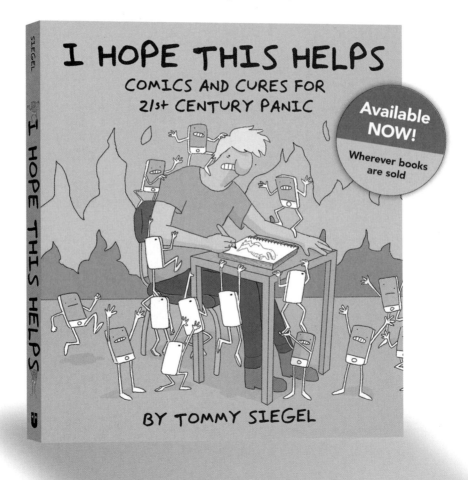

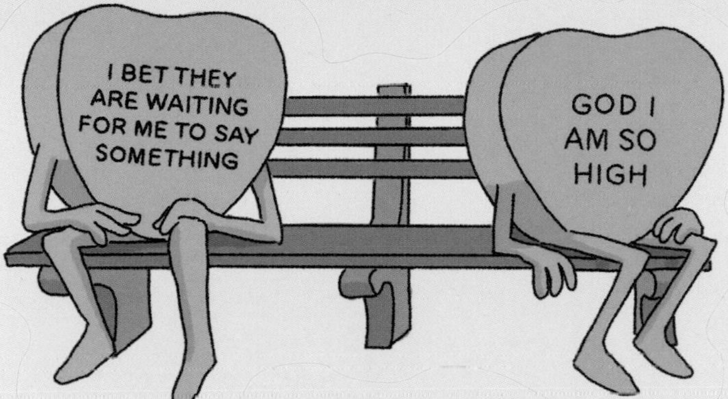
I BET THEY ARE WAITING FOR ME TO SAY SOMETHING
GOD I AM SO HIGH

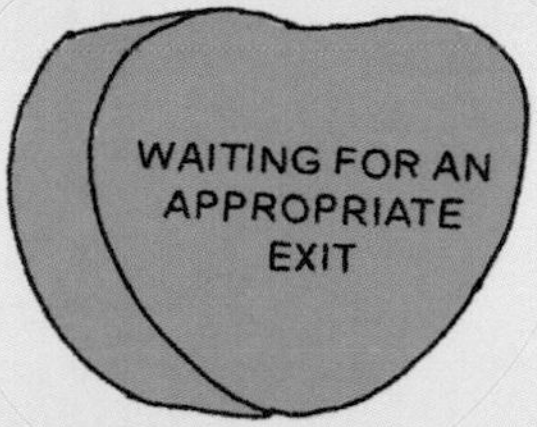
WAITING FOR AN APPROPRIATE EXIT

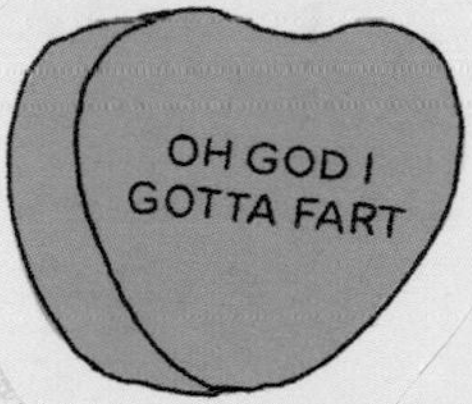
OH GOD I GOTTA FART

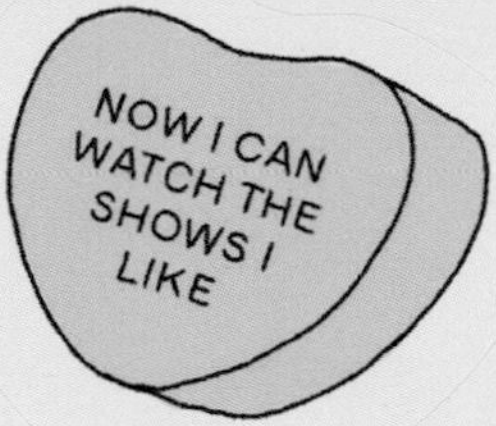
NOW I CAN WATCH THE SHOWS I LIKE

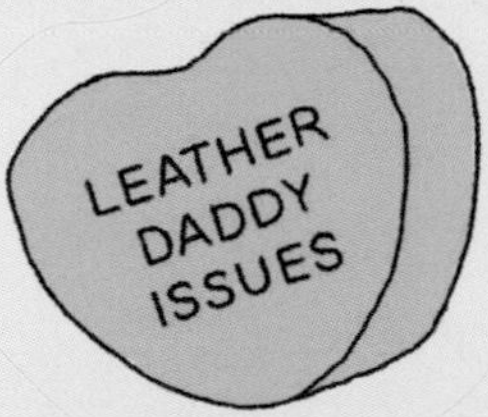
LEATHER DADDY ISSUES

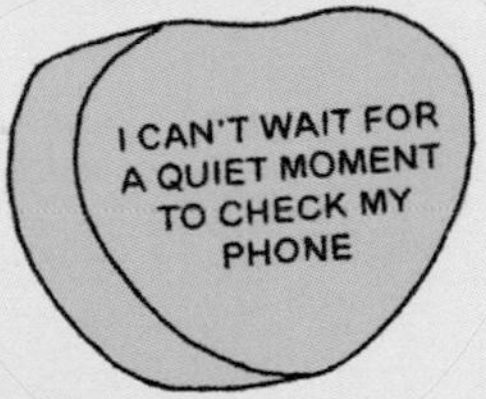
I CAN'T WAIT FOR A QUIET MOMENT TO CHECK MY PHONE

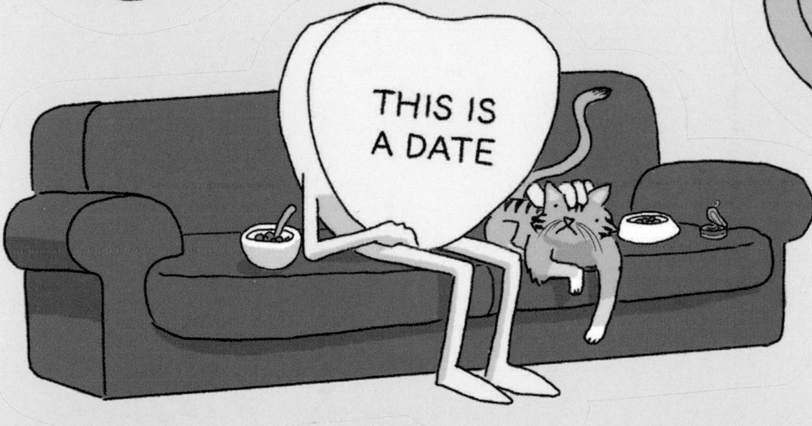
THIS IS A DATE

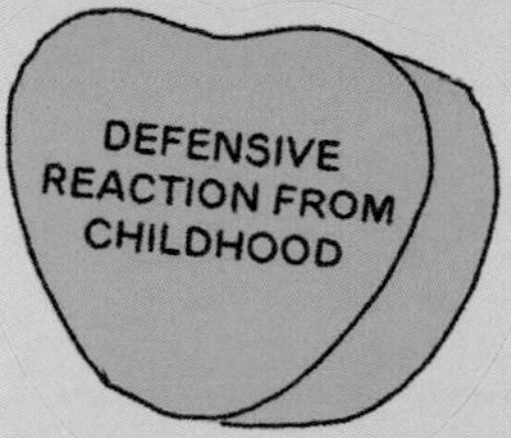
DEFENSIVE REACTION FROM CHILDHOOD

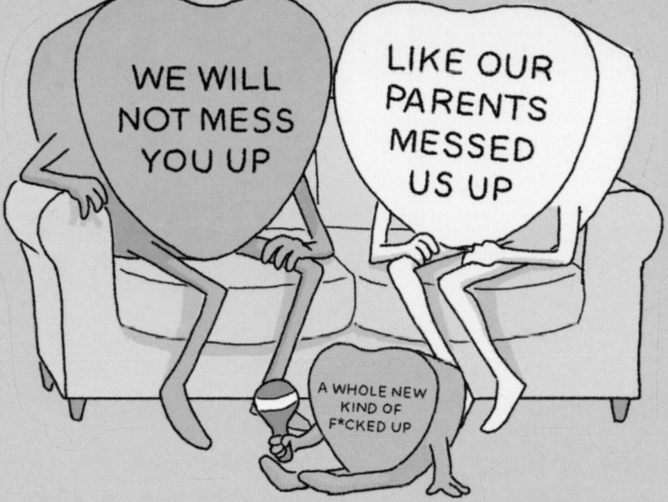
WE WILL NOT MESS YOU UP
LIKE OUR PARENTS MESSED US UP
A WHOLE NEW KIND OF F*CKED UP

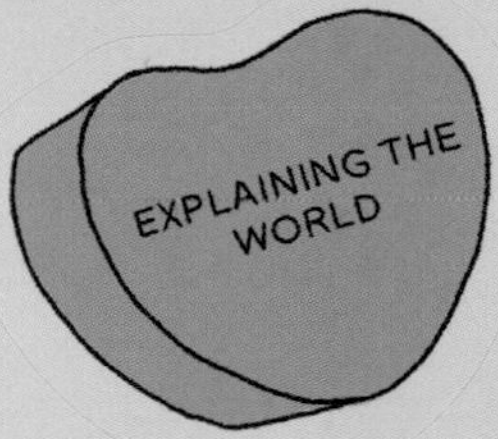
EXPLAINING THE WORLD

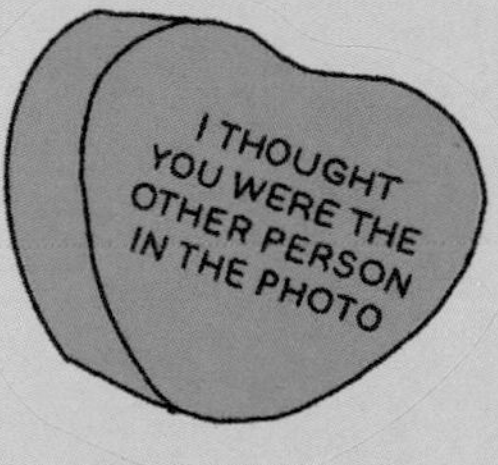
I THOUGHT YOU WERE THE OTHER PERSON IN THE PHOTO

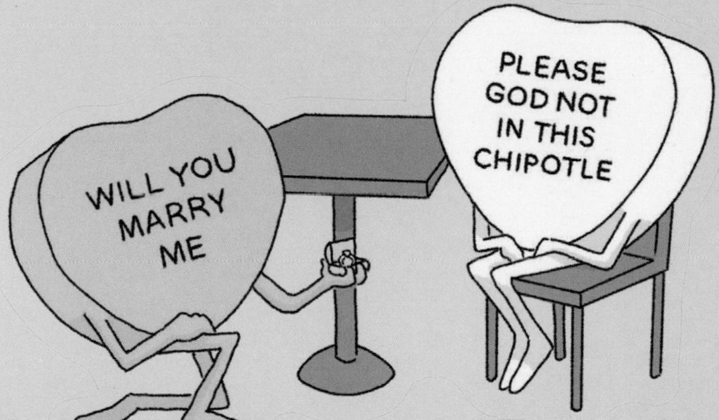
WILL YOU MARRY ME
PLEASE GOD NOT IN THIS CHIPOTLE

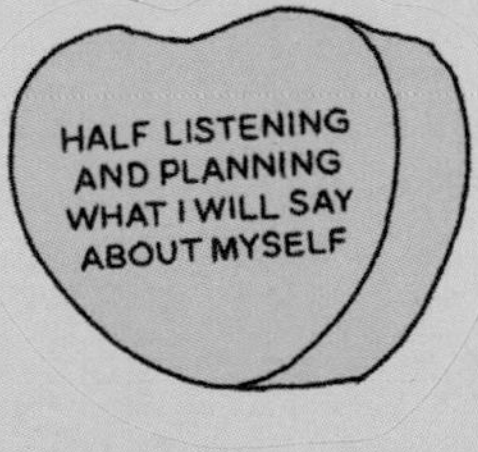
HALF LISTENING AND PLANNING WHAT I WILL SAY ABOUT MYSELF

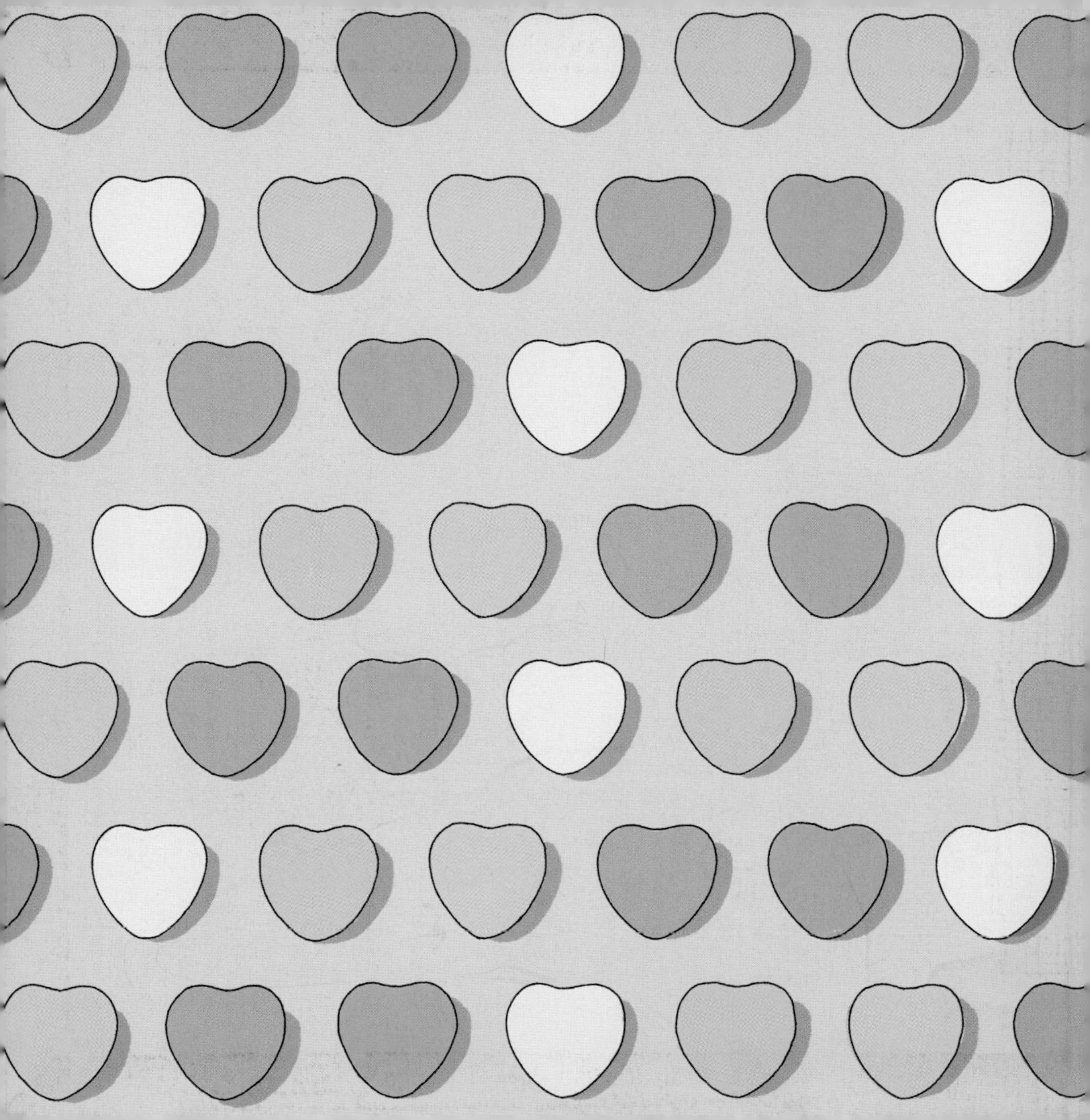